W9-BNE-645

# A New Owner's Guide to POODLES

JG-129

**Overleaf:** Toy Poodles owned by Patricia A. Zbock.

**Opposite page:** Standard Poodles owned by Carol A. Fale.

**The publisher wishes to acknowledge the following owners of the dogs in this book:** Naomi Acocella, DeWitt Bolden, Linda Brown and Bob Meissenheimer, Joan Brenneke, Deborah Butler, Neil Callahan, Meredith and James Carlson, Joan Carver, Scott and Karen Chamberlain, Rachel Cserni, Bob and Judy Dumond, Rosa Engler, Carol Fale, Sherrie Flynn, Linda Gambino, Linda Gemeinhardt, David Hershkowitz, Maryann K. Howarth, Cythnia Huff, Pam Hunt, Marilyn Imm, James Johnson, Doris Lilienthal, Honey Loring, Cheryl Ann Martin, Sandra Michel, Ronald and Sharon Morrison, Sandra Pearce, Dawn and Troy Phillips, Kimm Pontiff, Leslie Pope-Hall, Ellen S. Price, S. Seligman, Martin Simon, Lou Slzemore, Nicole Snow, La Mae Spaniolo, Nanci Takash, Beverly Walter, Pearl Wanner, Dorothy White, A. Gina Wieser, and Patricia Zbock.

**Photographers:** Dorothy Callahan, Carol Fale, Isabelle Francais, Yvonne Gamblin, Honey Loring, Sandra Michel, Paul Newman, Robert Pearcy, Photography by Sherry; Kimm Pontiff, Charlotte Schwartz, Nanci Takash, and Karen Taylor.

The author acknowledges the contribution of Judy Iby for the following chapters: Sport of Purebred Dogs, Identification and Finding the Lost Dog, Traveling with Your Dog, and Health Care for Your Dog.

T.F.H. Publications, Inc.
One TFH Plaza
Third and Union Avenues
Neptune City, NJ 07753



ISBN 0-7938-2778-7



www.tfh.com

# A New Owner's Guide to POODLES

Charlotte Schwartz

# Contents

**2003 Edition**



**A well-cared-for Poodle, like this white Standard, will be a healthy, loving companion for many years.**

**Poodles come in a variety of colors, including the apricot color of this Mini Poodle.**

Because he is an elegant, athletic dog, the Poodle can carry off the elaborate Continental Clip in which he is shown.

Poodles have a natural affinity for water. This one is happy in the pool.



Poodles are agile, intelligent dogs that love physical activities, like clearing hurdles on an agility course.

# Dedication

*To Brett and Ginger*
*You make the sun shine for me.*

# Preface

This book goes deep below the curly, coifed surface of the Poodle to focus on a most unique breed of dog. Developed hundreds of years ago, the Poodle hasn't changed much from when he was first recognized as a happy, willing companion to mankind.

In the book, I offer a descriptive comparison of the three sizes of Poodle: Toy, Miniature, and Standard. I touch briefly on the history of the Poodle to give the reader a proper perspective on what makes the breed tick.

I also offer some thoughts on the matter of canine intellect. Poodles are alert and vocal, not silent and serious as some of their working class cousins. They're so versatile and smart, they're often called the most intelligent breed.

The standard of the breed is discussed in a "word picture" of what a Poodle should look like. I offer suggestions on selecting, caring for, and training a Poodle. Sporting events for Poodles, traveling, health care, and housetraining are addressed as well.

Finally, I introduce you to some interesting Poodles that sell the breed to all who know them.

Throughout the book, I've attempted to share my love and enthusiasm for Poodles without sugar-coating them in a barrage of over-exaggerated glorifications. I care too much about the breed to be anything less than honest.

# Acknowledgments

Can you imagine writing a book such as this without needing a whole chapter just to thank those who contributed to it? I can't! Now, I must try.

Unlike a novel or scholarly work, this book is about sharing—people sharing what they know and feel and think about a most wonderful breed of dog. I took what they shared with me and added my own experiences and thoughts. This is the end result. I hope its contents will enlighten you regarding Poodles—Toys, Miniatures, and Standards alike.

But there was more sharing to come—photographs taken by Poodle lovers who proudly present the versatility of their own dogs by way of pictures. In doing so, they made this analysis come to life for those interested and/or involved in Poodle ownership. Thank you one and all! You helped make this book a fair judgment of what Poodles are and are not. For my part, I present the pluses and minuses of the breed as I know them (and I've bred them, shown them, trained them, and loved them for far too long to admit).

Now, after all the facts are considered, I ask you to decide whether you're willing enough, smart enough, patient enough, and enthusiastic enough to live with a Poodle.

To my editors, Jaime Gardner and Andrew De Prisco, I extend sincere gratitude for guiding me along the way and for organizing my materials into a most attractive volume. They knew I love Poodles. They believed I'd be fair in my assessment. I've tried not to disappoint them.

Charlotte Schwartz

*Part of what makes Poodles so popular is that they come in all different sizes and colors. Pictured here is a gray Standard.*

# INTRODUCTION

Welcome to the world of Poodles. Getting to know this fascinating breed of dog is a lot like going to a big party. There'll be all kinds of characters there. You'll see handsome males; beautiful, elegant females; chubby, round youngsters; even adorable babies. You'll see enough shapes, sizes, and colors to boggle your mind. Colors as brilliant as virgin snow, dusty beige to Irish Setter red, subtle gray-blues, and the black of an onyx.

You'll meet princely scholars, sovereign leader-types, charming females who make you feel you've known them forever, bouncy adolescents overflowing with the love of life. The babies will captivate you with their "pick me up and cuddle me" looks. You'll see dowagers wanting only a moment of quiet reverie. And, of course, no party would be complete without party animals—clowns, tricksters, acrobats, and dancers who add zest to any gathering.

So come along with me as we investigate this unique breed of dog. We'll examine the three different sizes of Poodle, their myriad colors, and why they look the way they do. We'll learn about the original purpose of the breed and how that ancestral intent influences Poodles even today.

Throughout this book you'll meet some fascinating individuals and discover just how diversified Poodles can be. Then, following your journey of discovery, you may decide that there is one particular Poodle just right for you.

# HISTORY of the Poodle

Because we often hear the breed referred to as "French Poodles," it seems reasonable to assume that the breed originated in France. After all, Rhodesian Ridgebacks came from Rhodesia and Norwegian Elkhounds originated in Norway. However, that assumption would be incorrect.

Actually, the breed is so ancient that it goes back in antiquity to the Middle Ages, more specifically the 15th century, when it began appearing in Roman art and writings. Going even further back in time than that, there were pictures of poodle-like dogs carved on Roman tombs and Greek coins in the 12th century. But since no one has been able to prove the Poodle's origin, historians have come to the conclusion that, as far as modern Poodles are concerned, the breed probably originated in Germany, France, and Russia simultaneously.

*The Poodle is an ancient breed whose coat has always inspired a style of its own. This Poodle is corded, which was particularly fashionable at the turn of the century.*

In Germany, they were called pudel dogs. Translated, the word "pudel" means to splash in water. The dogs were heavier-boned than those in France and Russia, yet they all possessed a strong desire to retrieve. It was also in Germany that Poodles were found with two types of coat: the curly or woolly and the corded. The corded variety, however, was short-lived, as maintaining a coat that hung in hundreds of long cords was simply too difficult to manage and keep clean. In addition, when the corded coats got wet, they stayed that way for days on end.

The Russian Poodle was taller, more refined, and very

*This Standard Poodle would probably not recognize his taller and more refined ancient Russian ancestor.*

similar to a Greyhound in appearance. The French dogs were more fine-boned than those from Germany and were called Chien Canne or Caniche (duck dog).

The various names given to these dogs is an important clue to the purpose for which they were originally bred. First we find that, in every country, they were good retrievers. Their love of carrying things in their mouths meant that they could be easily trained to retrieve fallen upland game—pheasant, grouse, and quail—for hunters. Add to that their love of swimming and you have a dog that can be taught to retrieve ducks downed over water.

Originally, hunting was not a sport but a means to provide meat for the table. Throughout the Middle Ages, large Poodles, mostly of the Standard size, proved to be worthy assistants to their masters on the hunt. It was during this time that the long, heavy coats of the Poodle became a serious problem. On land they functioned exceedingly well, but once in the water the density of those woolly coats soaked up water like a sponge and the dogs frequently drowned as they swam back to shore with the fallen game birds.

Hunters had to find a way to lighten the dogs once they were water borne. And they did. They shaved away all unnecessary hair into what became known as the lion cut. A blanket of hair covering the chest area protected the heart and lungs from icy waters. Leg joints were protected by sculpting pompons around each joint. In short, all hair that did not serve a protective purpose was shaved away. The face, feet, sides, back, hips, and thighs were kept clean. Even the tail, which was left much longer in those early days, was shaved with the exception of a tuft at the tip.

Today, in breed ring competition around the world, those same styles—with the exception of the puppies, that may be shown in what is known as the puppy clip—are mandatory cuts for all Poodles regardless of size. Pet Poodles and those participating in sporting activities are a different story. They're usually groomed in more simplified styles because the plainer cuts are easier to create and maintain.

I often hear people comment that they do not wish to own Poodles because of the dogs elaborate styles. This remark always prompts me to explain the why and how of Poodle grooming, thus diffusing erroneous opinions. The *puppy clip*, for example, allows Poodles under one year of age to be shown with full coats. However,

*An excellent retriever and natural water dog, the fleet-footed Poodle's first job was to assist man on the hunt.*

*Gigi, a white Miniature, shows off a lovely pet clip, complete with bows over her ears.*

the face, feet, and base of tail are shaved. The body coat may be trimmed to create a smooth, well-shaped appearance.

In the *English saddle clip*, a short blanket of hair is permitted to remain over the hindquarters. If this style is chosen by the owner for showing the dog, a superb grooming job is a must.

The *Continental clip* varies from the English saddle only in the hindquarters. The hindquarters are shaved clean with the exception of a sculpted pompon over each hip. This style exposes the entire rear half of the dog to the eye of the judge. Therefore, the Continental clip should be used only with dogs possessing near perfect conformation.

In all Poodle clips, the hair of the topknot (the hair over the top of the skull) may be left to fall freely or may be held back from the face with a rubber band.

Understanding the various types of clips used on Poodles and the reasons behind them usually clears up misconceptions about the breed. After all, the hunters of the Middle Ages were probably as strong and virile a group as any modern man, and their hunting dogs would hardly have been considered weak.

The Poodle's intelligence and eagerness to please were not lost, it seems, on those other than hunters. During the 16th, 17th, and 18th centuries, people began breeding smaller-sized Standard Poodles together to create what we know today as the Miniature Poodle. Following that, the Petit Barbet, or Toy Poodle, was developed.

These smaller versions of the original Standard Poodle held a wide range of jobs as companions to people. Miniature Poodles were formed into dancing troupes that entertained the ladies of the courts. In addition, Miniature Poodle acts criss-crossed the European countryside to amuse the commoners who were never a part of the aristocracy. Medium-sized Poodles were equally as trainable as Standards, yet easier to maintain in groups and transport around the country.

*The athletic Poodle is an ideal sportsman and crowd pleaser. This Poodle easily glides over a bar jump in an obedience competition.*

*Toy Poodles were once referred to as "Sleeve Poodles" because they could fit into their mistresses' dress sleeves.*

Miniature Poodles are agile little dogs, extremely intelligent and acrobatic, and they possess large egos. As such, they absolutely adore attention and applause and will perform for hours for an appreciative audience. Those characteristics are still as strong in the Poodle today as they were in the earlier centuries.

When the smallest Miniature Poodles were bred together, we saw the emergence of the Toy Poodle. However, those typically endearing Poodle traits were not sacrificed by breeders when they created the diminutive Toy Poodle. Though not as easy to develop, the Toy soon came into great demand. They were often referred to as "Sleeve Poodles," and for very good reason.

Toy Poodles were favored by female fanciers and so small that they could travel easily with their owners without hampering the activities of the ladies. With their typical Poodle characteristics of intelligence, willingness to please, and eagerness to socialize with humans, Toy Poodles were ideal companions for the ladies of France.

In addition, the French affinity for style in clothes and hairdos made Toy Poodles perfect candidates for frequent groomings. With shaven feet and faces, the dogs carried almost no dirt to the clothes or homes of their owners.

Toy Poodles were so popular that, in the late 1700s, King Louis XVI of France commissioned the famous painter Francisco de Goya to create a portrait of his wife Marie Antoinette's Toy Poodles. Today, the Poodle is considered the national dog of France.

By the 18th century, Toy Poodles were establishing themselves in Great Britain as well. They accompanied their mistresses to afternoon teas, sat on their laps when the ladies entertained, and reinforced the nickname of "Sleeve Poodles." During the 18th and 19th centuries, Poodles grew in popularity and were frequently the subjects of art and literature. In the mid-19th century, for example, Sir Edwin Landseer, a favorite artist of British royalty, memorialized the breed in his paintings.

*This relative of the Poodle is a Lagotto Truffle Dog from Italy. Small Poodles are used as Truffle Dogs because of their keen sense of smell and light step.*

Regarding the Poodle's earliest beginnings, some historians believe that the English Water Dog, now extinct, contributed to the development of the Poodle. Still others believe that the Poodle, with his distinctive curly coat, was responsible for the development of the English Water Dog.

While the spaniel may have contributed to the origin of the Poodle, we see that the Toy Poodle contributed to the creation of the Truffle Dog. Little dogs trained to track down and unearth the underground fungus known

*This black Miniature hopes to follow in the footsteps of the first Mini to win a championship, Ch. Chieveley Chopstick.*

throughout England and France as a delicacy, Truffle Dogs were probably a cross of Toy Poodles and terriers. Since truffle gathering is done at night, the tiny white dogs were easier to see in the dark and lighter of foot, which prevented them from crushing the fungus. Poodles also possess excellent scenting ability, making it easier for them to locate truffles.

Whether Poodles were used in the creation of some spaniel breeds or some spaniel breeds were used in the development of Poodles remains unclear. And we will probably never know the exact circumstances and progenitors of Poodles. However, we do know that once mankind identified the special qualities and traits that made the Poodle a desirable companion, Poodle breeding became an accepted practice in Europe, Great Britain, and finally, America.

Poodles found their way to America as early as 1887,but it wasn't until just before World War I that Poodle popularity became a reality. In those early days of Poodles in America, Standards and Miniatures were exhibited in the dog show ring as a single breed. They were divided, however, by type of coat: the curly and the corded.

Toys, almost always white back in those days, were shown as a distinctly different breed. It wasn't until after World War II that the

Poodle Club of America, founded in 1931 as the governing body for the breed, offered classes for the Toy variety with the same criteria as Miniatures and Standards except for size.

The first Miniature to win a champion title was a black English import named Ch. Chieveley Chopstick. During that time, Eric Labory of Misty Isles, a black Standard of German breeding, was imported from the well-known Labory Kennel in Switzerland.

In 1933, another handsome black Standard, Ch. Whippendell Poli of Carillon, won the Non-Sporting Group at the prestigious Westminster Kennel Club show in New York City.

Then, in 1935, a white Standard import named Ch. Nunsoe Duc de la Terrace of Blakeen went all the way to the top of dogdom by winning Best in Show at the Westminster Kennel Club show in Madison Square Garden. Duc's handler and

*In 1935, a white Standard Poodle won Best in Show at the prestigious Westminster Kennel Club.*

*Despite his elaborate appearance, the Poodle is very agile and can excel in a variety of sporting events.*

owner, Mrs. Hayes Blake Hoyt, was also the first woman to reach the Best in Show winner's circle at Westminster.

Poodle popularity continued to grow and these early winners contributed significantly to the gene pools of future winners in all three Poodle sizes. By 1960, Poodles were the most popular breed of dog in American Kennel Club records. They have been at or near the top of the popularity chart ever since.

## Poodles in Obedience

A satellite activity open to all purebred dogs and particularly favored by Poodle owners undoubtedly helped to maintain the breed's popularity over the long haul. Obedience competition is the name of the game.

It all began back in the 1930s. Mrs. Helene Whitehouse Walker, owner of Carillon Kennels and breeder of top-winning Standard Poodles, became disheartened at the idea that her beloved Poodles weren't taken seriously by her friends because of their style of grooming. She knew that her dogs were equal, if not superior, in intelligence to

*Loyal and obedient, the Poodle takes his role as friend and family companion very seriously.*

most of the working and sporting breeds. She also knew that with no obedience testing open to Poodles at the time she'd have to create a test to prove her theory once and for all.

So in 1934, Mrs. Walker went to England where obedience was a growing sport. She studied dog training methods with some of the country's top trainers. When she returned to America, she enlisted the aid of a friend, Blanch Saunders, to help in the campaign for all-breed obedience. Until that time, only sporting and working dogs were trained in obedience and the training was used primarily for protection and field trial work.

Mrs. Walker taught Ms. Saunders everything she'd learned in England and soon Blanch Saunders became one of America's first-rate obedience instructors. Not long after that, they formed America's first dog training club, the Obedience Test Club of New York. Shortly afterward, the OTC of New York joined forces with the North Westchester (NY) Kennel Club to offer the first all-breed obedience test at a dog show.

At the beginning of World War II, the Obedience Test Club was disbanded. In 1941, the American Kennel Club finally recognized the New England Dog Training Club as the first AKC affiliated obedience club. That event opened the way for all purebred dogs to earn such titles as Companion Dog, Companion Dog Excellent, and Utility Dog. Today, the sport includes two additional obedience titles: Utility Dog Excellent and Obedience Trial Champion.

By 1947, a set of standards for judging obedience tests was put to use at all AKC trials. Finally, in 1972, the American Kennel Club officially adopted the obedience regulations and formed a separate obedience department with Richard D'Ambrisi as its first director.

Today, Poodle owners by the thousands enjoy training their dogs for obedience competition and the ultimate goal of achieving the various titles. With their penchant for pleasing their owners, jumping, retrieving, performing, and socializing, Poodles have proved their worth as successful sportsmen. This then adds another dimension to their relationship with man.

# CHARACTERISTICS of the Poodle

In a world that offers several hundred breeds of dog for potential companionship, the Poodle is probably the most unique breed of all. Just think about it. Poodles come in sizes ranging from 3 pounds to 75 or 80 pounds. Their sizes are specified as Toy, Miniature, and Standard. Their colors create a rainbow of canine hues. They are among only a handful of breeds that do not shed or carry a body odor. And that's just a smattering of the qualities that endear them to humans.

Let's examine some of the others. Take intelligence, for example. Poodle owners are often heard to proclaim that their dogs are the most intelligent breed. However, making such a broad statement may be unwise and unfair to all breeds of dog, including the Poodle.

Before we decide whether or not it is an accurate statement, we need to clarify the meaning of intelligence. Intelligence is defined as the capacity to understand and reason. In other words, it's the ability to *recall the past* (the dog remembers that a particular person struck him), *act in the present* (the dog runs away when the person attempts to strike him again), and *anticipate the future* (the dog completely avoids the person in the future).

*The well-groomed Poodle is known for his keen intelligence and high level of trainability.*

Here's another example, this one of a positive nature. *Recall the past*—the puppy picks up a tennis ball with his mouth. *Act in the present*—you wit-ness the event and call the puppy to you, where-upon you take the ball and tell him "What a good boy you are!" You also pet him excitedly and laugh aloud. *Anticipate the future*—later, the

*Poodles are one of only a few breeds that do not shed or have a body odor, which means you may not even notice if they sit on the furniture!*

puppy sees the ball, recalls the event and how you responded to him. He enjoyed the praise and wants more of it, so he repeats the behavior hoping that his fetch will bring yet another celebration.

Intellect, then, is the faculty of the mind by which a dog understands, solves problems, and adapts to new situations. Put another way, it's the ability of the mind by which a dog knows and behaves adaptively as opposed to emotionally.

In this context, all dogs can reason to some extent and all can understand to some degree. Perhaps they can't reach the intellectual heights of humankind, but they can learn. This we know, and most dogs prove it every day.

On the surface, then, it appears that what a dog knows determines how smart he or she is. However, to be accurate in our judgment of intellect, we must go deeper into our study of canine intelligence. That brings us to genetic engineering.

In their comprehensive study at Bar Harbor, Maine, and their subsequent book entitled *Genetics and the Social Behavior of Dogs*,

Drs. John Scott and John Fuller found that all breeds of dog seem to be very much the same in intelligence. What is different about the various breeds is that each breed is genetically engineered for specific behaviors, making them extremely proficient at those tasks while seemingly not able to excel at others. In other words, dogs are genetic specialists.

Take the Komondor, for example. Komondors are genetically engineered to be fearless protectors of flocks of sheep. As such, they live their lives in the open with the sheep rather than in the homes of the herdsmen.

Afghan Hounds specialize in independence, not subordination. They're good at coursing (racing after) large hares and mountain deer. As independent hunters, they're bred to work for man, not with him.

In both cases, a high degree of self-reliance is necessary for their survival. A Komondor that can't guard sheep or an Afghan that can't catch prey would not be used for breeding. Therefore, if all Komondors and Afghans failed at the purposes for which they were bred, the breeds would eventually become extinct.

In addition, Drs. Scott and Fuller found that a dog will perform a certain task well in a situation where he becomes highly motivated,

*Dogs will be dogs—your Poodle will have the same inherited tendencies and behavioral characteristics as his working ancestors.*

*Matthew Fale snuggles with his puppy, Kelsey.*

providing he has the physical capacity to do so. Couple motivation and physical capability with the genes necessary to perform a specific job and you have a breed that possesses a high degree of intelligence for specific behaviors.

Thus, for hundreds of years, breeders have deliberately bred for the traits they deemed desirable in their chosen breeds, thereby creating genetic specialists. In each case and within each specialty, the dogs are considered highly intelligent.

Why some breeds appear to be more intelligent than others, then, seems more related to what they understand rather than to how they understand. Therein lies the secret to canine intelligence, and that secret appears to come as much from their genes as their brains. In other words, intelligence is breed-specific in dogs.

For example, Poodles have been bred for hundreds of years to be dependent on human companions. They do not function well alone. Instead they need to be with, work for, and please their masters. In turn, humans have used this need to its fullest potential.

Poodles are athletic, active, curious, social, and capable of mentally focusing on human behavior in order to learn. In addition, they have large egos. Once they discover that a specific behavior brings human approval, they will perform it for hours on end just for the attention it brings.

All dogs are capable of experiencing a wide range of emotions similar to those of humans. Poodles, however, are exceptionally

*The versatile Poodle enjoys many outdoor activities, including leisurely boat rides with his family.*

*Playful and energetic, Poodles were once famous for their roles as captivating circus performers.*

perceptive in recognizing our emotions whether we express them covertly or openly.

Despite the fact that their main purpose today is no longer to retrieve fallen ducks, they still carry the genes for retrieving. Consequently, they've evolved into dogs that love to carry things, all sorts of things, in their mouths. Again, mankind uses this trait to his advantage for both useful and entertainment purposes.

To even the most casual observer, Poodles carry themselves with a certain dignity. They are dedicated to their owners yet they love other people, too. They're playful and exhibit a keen sense of humor that sparkles from their bright eyes at every opportunity. In short, they love life.

Finally, their physiological makeup, or how their bodies are constructed, allows them to perform often amazing feats of dexterity and balance. It was this feature that made Poodles such captivating circus performers years ago.

Keeping in mind the theory of genetic engineering, we see that Poodles are specialists at not one or two traits, but at many. All of these aspects—intellect, genetic engineering, physical abilities, and emotional intuitiveness—combine to create a dog of great versatility.

No wonder, then, that Poodles are referred to as the most intelligent breed.

## Physical Traits

In addition to excelling at a multitude of behavioral traits, Poodles are deliberately bred to look a certain way. Whether the dog is a Toy, Miniature, or Standard, the Poodle must meet a particular physical description identical to all others of his breed regardless of size.

Throughout the world there are national breed clubs that have set standards of perfection to determine what is and what is not acceptable in the physical conformation of the Poodle. In the United States, that club is the Poodle Club of America.

For now, let's get a general overview of what Poodles are all about.

The only difference in the three varieties of Poodles is size. Standards must be over 15 inches from the top of the withers (shoulders) to the ground. Miniatures are over 10 inches and under 15 inches from the withers, and Toys are to be 10 inches and under.

The dog, regardless of size, should appear to be squarely built. In other words, it should be as tall from the withers to the ground as it is long from the tip of the breastbone to the rump (buttocks).

*Regardless of size or color, Poodles are bred to look a certain way, which is accentuated in the show ring.*

The eyes should be dark, oval in shape, and present an intelligent alertness. Round and/or protruding eyes are major faults.

The skull is slightly rounded and the muzzle should be long, straight, and refined. Ears should begin slightly below the level of the eyes and hang close to the head. The teeth should have a scissors bite, while overshot or undershot jaws are unacceptable.

Fore and hindquarters should be well muscled and in proportion to the size of

*Nine-month-old Tarra has a puppy clip that shows off her long, straight muzzle and small, oval feet.*

the dog. Feet should be rather small, oval, and have well-arched toes.

The Poodle should be double coated. The top coat should be wiry, thick, and curly while the undercoat should be soft and woolly to provide warmth. In puppies, however, all of the hair is soft and fine. The adult wiry coat begins to emerge as the dog matures. When considering a puppy's future coat, look to his parents to predict what kind of coat he will likely have as an adult.

It is this combination of hair that lends itself so well to such a wide variety of grooming styles. The pet Poodle owner has, many choices in deciding his dog's hairstyle. Professional groomers everywhere offer such styles known as utility cuts, sporting clips, puppy clips, and so forth. In addition, there are many regionally popular clips chosen by owners for convenience and simplicity in daily coat care.

For example, dogs living in the colder regions of the North are often groomed with longer coats for protection from the elements. In the tropics, Poodles are frequently seen with their bodies shaved very short and only pompons on their hips, ankles, wrists, and top knots. This style makes it easy for owners to guard against fleas and ticks.

Poodles destined for the conformation show ring are allowed one of two choices. The English Saddle and the Continental clips are the only two styles permitted on adult dogs. Puppies under one year of age may be shown in the puppy clip where only the face, feet, and base of tail are clipped. The body may be slightly scissored in order to present a neat unbroken line and to create a pleasant appearance.

The topknot (hair on the top of the skull) on show dogs may be left to fall freely or kept in place with a rubber band. In both cases, the hair should be managed to create a smooth line from the head to the body. Dogs in pet clips, however, almost always have their topknots scissored into a pompon on the top of the head.

As for color, no other breed of dog offers as much choice to the potential buyer. We begin with the traditional black and white and move quickly to gray. That opens up a wide range of shades from light silvery gray to a deep rich gunmetal gray that is sometimes referred to as blue.

Many years ago, I bought a blue Standard Poodle as a companion for my grandson, Brett. As Jeanne developed into a charming mature adult, she and Brett worked together in obedience and finally as members of an exhibition team. When Jeanne died at age 12, she was still that lovely shade of gunmetal blue.

Chocolate brown can be strikingly rich and deep like dark chocolate and proceed down to a soft cafe au lait. From there we go to apricot, which is bright and orangey. It is common in some areas, while very rare in other parts of the world.

The creams range in shades from the aforementioned cafe au lait to the palest of pale. At a distance, the pale cream dog may appear to be white, but on close inspection, we see that the ears may be a few shades darker and the nose, eye-rims, and lips are liver colored. The eyes may be a dark amber rather than the traditional black.

Puppies are frequently born darker in color and lighten as they mature. My own Ginger, a 12-inch Miniature, was a deep apricot at 8 weeks of age but now, at 8 years of age, she has mellowed out to be a luscious shade of butterscotch.

Because Poodles don't shed their hair, it continues to grow similar to the way human hair does. Grooming, therefore, becomes a major issue with this breed. Anyone who is considering acquiring a Poodle must accept the responsibility of frequent grooming as part of life with a Poodle. Neglecting the grooming process often produces a good deal of discomfort and unhappiness for both dog and owner. Done frequently, however, it does not become a great burden—in fact, most Poodles learn to love being groomed!

## STANDARDS

Now we turn our attention to the several similarities and differences in the three sizes of Poodle. We begin with the Standard Poodle. Imagine, if you will, a large, elegant, well-groomed, agile dog that displays pride and dignity in every step he takes. With head and tail held high, he struts out almost as if he were prancing to the beat of a lively tune. Walking behind such a creature, the Poodle owner soon discovers that, unlike any other breed of dog, the Poodle (the Standard in particular) has a swagger to his gait that invites admiration from all who see him.

The happy demeanor of his body and the intelligent expression on his face promise fun and friendship to everyone he meets. Even the smallest youngster rarely shows fear of a sound-minded Standard for more than a minute. He has a special way about him that bespeaks kindness and trust.

However, the Standard Poodle can be a formidable presence when he feels all is not right in his environment. The massive chest

*Poodles are eye-catching because of their looks and the dignified way they carry themselves—even at play.*

*Only a dog with character and poise can carry off such an elaborate hairstyle and make it look elegant.*

contains a deep growl and a threatening bark that can be heard for a great distance. His size backs up his promise to take charge of a potential problem.

For the past 30 years, I have lived with a variety of Standard Poodles and not once in all that time has my home or my family been threatened or violated. For the person in search of a large watchdog that doesn't shed, there is only one dog that meets that criterion—the Standard Poodle.

### Miniatures

The quick, vivacious, "Mr. Personality" Miniature Poodle is perhaps the most popular of the three sizes. He's big enough to hold up to an owner's physically active lifestyle and he's small enough to sleep in a compact wire or fiberglass crate when the family travels.

His medium size allows him to be handled by adults and children alike. Many older people who are reluctant to attempt living with a dog as strong as a Standard Poodle will readily accept the comfort and civility offered by a Miniature Poodle. A lady I know switched from owning Standards to Miniatures during later years of her life saying, "The Mini is like a scaled-down version of my Standards, and the smaller ones take only half the time to brush out everyday."

Miniature Poodles make excellent alarm dogs, drawing themselves up to full height as they bark a warning when they feel something is amiss or when a stranger is approaching. Having a dog that barks is extremely effective since unwanted visitors do not want to draw attention to themselves.

As a child, I lived on a farm and we had many medium-sized dogs that lived there with us. One of my father's favorite sayings was, "I keep medium-sized dogs on the place to bark. I just want them to sound a warning: We'll do the biting!"

One additional feature of the Miniature Poodle relates to our modern day lifestyles. As housing space grows less abundant and the cost of private homes increases, many people are choosing to live in apartments and condominiums. Often the policies of these facilities state that small and medium dogs are acceptable and that large dogs are not. Many condominium documents are even more specific and clearly state that dogs over 25 or 30 pounds are considered too large and are not permitted to live in those units. Once again, Miniature Poodles meet the criterion.

*The vivacious Miniature Poodle is often called "Mr. Personality." His small size and charisma have earned him tremendous popularity.*

## TOYS

Finally, we come to the diminutive Toy Poodle. These dogs fill very special niches in their owners' lives. Bred to be tiny, they can be carried just about everywhere their owners go. Planes, trains, cars, and hotels present no problem in accommodations.

A lady client of mine carries a pretty canvas bag over her shoulder whenever she goes shopping. If you saw her, you'd never think she had a dog with her, yet look inside that bag and you'd spot an adorable white Toy Poodle enjoying his trip to the mall as much as his mistress.

The Toy Poodle is an important breed for several other groups of people as well. People who live in big cities and do not want to walk their dogs alone at night appreciate Toy Poodles because they can easily be trained to relieve themselves on absorbent pads in a laundry or

*Because of their small sizes, Toy Poodles make great pets for people who live in large cities or who aren't physically capable of handling a medium- to large-sized dog.*

*The smart, happy-go-lucky Poodle is the dog for you if you love life and are willing to give this dog the quality time it deserves.*

bathroom. Very elderly people who want the companionship of a dog, yet are not physically able to handle even a medium-sized dog recognize the pleasure of owning a tiny Toy Poodle.

## Poodle Ownership

Who, then, makes the ideal owner for a Poodle? Based on the special features of each of the three sizes of Poodle, a person who enjoys an intelligent, active, and willing dog makes a potentially good Poodle owner. The owner must also recognize and accept the responsibility of frequent grooming whether he or she decides to groom the dog at home or have it done professionally.

Consider your own lifestyle and choose the Poodle that fits into it the best. Think about your own personality and pick the adult or puppy that compliments the way you see life. Poodles are very adaptable and mirror your image with exceptional ease. If you love life, like to laugh, enjoy other people, and are active (that could mean doing things around the home or getting out in the big world), a Poodle will be the perfect companion.

# SPECIAL ROLES of Today's Poodle

I have compared being in the company of Poodles to attending a party—there's something there for everyone, including all shapes, sizes and personalities. I hinted at some of the types of Poodles we'd see there and offered clues to the fascinating things they do in today's world. Now I'd like to introduce you to some specific Poodles that are living examples of those things.

In my search for Poodles of great diversity, I found a wonderful lady in Hot Springs, Arkansas. Her name is Carol Fale and her life with Poodles is a party every day. Let me tell you about some of the individuals with whom she shares her home.

Currently, Carol and her husband Randy live with three white Standard Poodles: Kelsey, and Kelsey's two daughters, Sousa and Roseanne. Kelsey and Sousa are both breed champions. Kelsey has earned a Companion Dog degree in obedience and a Canine Good Citizen title. Sousa has also earned a CGC title and participates in

*Carol Fale's Poodles are party animals and love the attention they get from their admirers.*

*If you laugh with them, Poodles will love to get dressed up for you.*

flyball races. Roseanne, on the other hand, prefers to live a quieter type of life at home with her family and out of the spotlight of breed ring competition and sporting events.

All of the Fale Poodles live in the house and share their home with Maggie, Randy's faithful Brittany, a hunting dog from the spaniel group. Carol has bred, groomed, and trained Poodles for 25 years. She does, however, engage a professional handler whenever her dogs are shown in the breed ring for conformation.

In the past, she owned Tara, a white Standard who earned a Utility Dog title and played flyball. Then there were two Miniature Poodles, Meg and Muffit. Whitney, a black Standard, was a breed champion with a CD degree and a Therapy Dog that worked with Alzheimer patients. Today, Kelsey and Sousa continue that tradition as therapy dogs.

Not only is Carol a busy wife, mother of grown children, and Poodle fancier with all the work that implies, she is also an active member of the National Association of Dog Obedience Instructors. As such, she teaches obedience classes in both Hot Springs and

Little Rock, Arkansas. Yet somehow, she always finds time to enjoy life with her Poodles. She teaches them tricks, dresses them up in costumes for special events, and plays with them daily.

The Fale Poodles really do seem to be characters straight from a great party. Remember the female charmers? The reverie seekers? The clowns and acrobats? Regardless, they're all loving, intelligent, willing, and talented. If we could ask them what is the one thing they most enjoy doing, they'd probably answer in unison, "Going to a party!"

## Therapy Dogs

Let me assure you that living with a therapy dog is an exciting and rewarding experience. At one point in my long association with this remarkable breed, my black Standard Poodle, Bonnie, became a therapy dog. She had earned a Utility Dog title and had been active in visiting schools and homes for the elderly as part of an exhibition team from Brandy Lane Dog Training School in Mt. Holly, New Jersey.

One summer day, the team traveled to a lovely home for the aged in the hills outside Philadelphia, Pennsylvania. I'll never forget the day, the place, or what happened there.

The team performed tricks and demonstrated obedience routines on a manicured emerald lawn while the patients, most in wheelchairs, some with walkers, sat under a red and white striped tent.

Following the performance, we all shared iced tea and cookies under the tent while the residents spoke with the dogs' owners and petted the dogs. During refreshment time, I noticed a frail little octogenarian sitting all alone in a wheelchair. No one spoke to her and she seemed not to care to speak to her fellow residents or the team members. While everyone enjoyed the festivities, she sat silently watching the dogs as they mingled with their elderly hosts. The lady seemed totally removed from the whole affair, as if she weren't even there, her mind a million miles away.

Troubled by the woman's reserved and unusual behavior, I decided to take Bonnie over to visit her. Maybe she would warm up to my gentle friend. We stopped in front of the lady and I attempted to engage her in conversation. Bonnie stood before her and, tail wagging, looked the lady square in the eyes. Slowly the lady reached out a timid hand to pet the fluffy topknot. Bonnie turned her head slightly and gently licked the lady's hand. The old lady smiled cautiously and, in a weak trill of a voice, said, "You have a beautiful face. What's your name?"

"Her name is Bonnie," I said. The old lady repeated the name and continued to pet the dog. Within seconds, the frail patient began telling Bonnie about some of the Poodles she'd had in her life, each more precious than the one before, each more intelligent than any other dog in the neighborhood, each as elegant as the one before her now. It soon became obvious that the lady had no intention of speaking with me. She seemed quite content to have Bonnie's undivided attention. And that attention appeared much more satisfying than any she might receive from another human being.

*The Poodle's love of people and level of trainability make him an excellent candidate for therapy dog work.*

The visit lasted for perhaps ten minutes. Bonnie and the lady shared the precious moments of togetherness as if they were totally removed from the crowd and the gaiety of the party. Then suddenly the visit was over. The lady caressed my Poodle one more time and said, "I have to go now. Please come back."

As an attendant wheeled her away, the lady stole one last glance at Bonnie.

As Bonnie and I prepared to move along to another patient, a well-groomed lady of about 50 approached me and asked, "I saw you talking to the lady in the wheelchair. What did she say to you?"

I explained that the lady spoke only to Bonnie about some of the Poodles she had lived with as a young woman. The lady's eyes filled with tears as I spoke. She dabbed at them with a lacy white handkerchief and proceeded to tell me the story of her mother, the little old lady in the wheelchair.

Her mother had suffered a stroke four years before and had never spoken a word after that. Though she'd received the finest treatment that money could buy and the doctors were certain that the lady would be able to speak again, the little lady remained silent, locked within her world of memories. After several years of treatment and therapy, the woman had placed her mother in this beautiful home for the aged thinking there was little else to be done for her. They were not wrong. The old lady never did speak again—until that afternoon at the garden party.

Perhaps she chose to break her silence to Bonnie because the dog was nonjudgmental, loving, and very gentle. The reason really doesn't matter. Bonnie's velvet tongue and soft brown eyes had done what no one else had been able to do. For a few minutes, Bonnie had changed the old lady's heart rate, increased her blood flow, and drawn back the curtain of silence to allow memories of years gone by to be heard by those who would listen. For a brief while, the old lady communicated again, shared her thoughts. She was alive!

So what is it about this therapy work with dogs that's so wonderful anyway? Aside from a few brief visits from a dog, what do the patients gain from it? And what's in it for the medical staff, the dogs' owners, and especially the dogs themselves?

*The Poodle's friendly, intelligent expression wins him friends wherever he goes, including to nursing homes as a therapy dog.*

Usually, the most dramatic results occur in the patients. For many, it's as if a floodgate has opened and tons of water comes rushing through, taking with it the unspoken burdens and sadness that has consumed them for years.

Living in the sterile world of rehabilitation centers and hospitals, the patients often find themselves lost among those who speak in medical terms, think scientifically, and frequently forget that each

*Poodles love children and have helped many struggle through tough times or handicaps. The feeling is usually mutual.*

patient is a unique human being with feelings and emotions whose importance is lost to those directly responsible for their care and cure.

Enter therapy dogs. Dogs that naturally love people and the attention they offer; dogs who have been trained to be gentle, quiet, and loving; dogs that make no demands, no judgments on the patients; dogs that come only to visit, participate in some quiet interaction, and receive attention from the patients, many of whom have previously lived with and loved dogs of their own. Poodles of all three sizes are among the best in the business.

The antiseptic world of an institution quickly melts away as patient and dog connect with each other. Smiles creep across wrinkled faces, hands that can barely hold a teacup become strong and purposeful as they offer a tiny biscuit, hold a leash, or pet soft fur in exchange for love and attention.

In schools and homes for handicapped youngsters, children open up to therapy dogs. They begin talking despite the fact that long ago they withdrew into themselves for whatever reason. Autistic children learn to focus and function. Blind children learn about soft fur, warm tongues, wagging tails, and willing friends whose body language says, "Follow me and we'll investigate this world together." The dogs lift the children out of their own world and into a new and brighter one.

The medical staff is often surprised to see a patient's response to the dogs and they look anew at their evaluations of a patient's condition. And just as in the case of the little lady in Pennsylvania, the staff arranges to include therapy dogs in the lives of their patients on a regular and frequent basis.

And what of the dogs and their owners? What do they get out of all this?

As I said earlier, seeing your own dog bring happiness to a stranger, recognition to a blank face, movement to previously still limbs is often reward enough. Usually it's so rewarding that you, the owner, will want to repeat the experience again and again.

The dogs probably receive as much from the visits as the patients. Poodles especially love the attention it brings. They love getting out among people and going places, doing things. But most of all, expanding the dogs' worlds makes them infinitely

*Whether you train your Poodle for therapy work or obedience competition, it should be fun and rewarding for both dog and owner.*

*With its variety of obstacles to go through, agility is one of the Poodle's favorite activities.*

more interesting and responsive in their roles as life partners with their owners.

When you add it all up, you make a minimum investment and receive a windfall profit that just can't be compared to any other activity that owners and dogs can share. Therapy dogs take the meaning of "man's best friend" to new heights!

## Other Activities

While spotlighting some present-day Poodles that are participating in unique activities, I'd like to tell you about a Standard Poodle breeder I recently met. Her name is Sandy Dingfelder and together with her husband, Simon, she owns Bay Breeze Kennels in Florida.

Not long ago one of the Dingfelder puppies went to live with a man who is a paraplegic. Confined to a wheelchair, the man is raising his puppy to assist him in a myriad of ways. Once grown and trained, the Poodle will offer his owner a new level of personal independence.

The dog will be trained to open doors, turn light switches on and off, retrieve dropped articles from the floor, fetch a phone receiver from its base, carry a bag of personal items when the owner travels, and remove clothing from dresser drawers. The dog will be taught to help his owner in whatever area of assistance the man deems necessary. In short, the dog will become the epitome of the word "partner."

In 1995, The Dingfelders sent yet another Poodle puppy to Germany where he will be trained as a guide dog for a blind person. Until recently, Poodles were thought to be inappropriate for guide dog work simply because of their grooming requirements. After all, a blind person would find it almost impossible to keep a Poodle well groomed. However, when a blind person lives with other adults, the sighted members of the household can keep the dog groomed while the dog serves as the eyes of the blind member.

Perhaps not as unique in their role as helpers yet certainly as important, there are hundreds of Poodles around the world who serve mankind. Let's look at some of the interesting and important work they do.

Take handy dogs, for example. Each dog lives with and assists a person who is handicapped in some way. Consequently, each dog is trained individually to perform specific tasks required by his owner.

Some act as ears for deaf people, some help to stabilize a person with a wobbly gait, and others carry things for an owner who uses crutches. Many serve to combat the loneliness of owners who live alone, yet others perform tasks for people whose bodies are disabled by arthritis and other debilitating diseases.

Consider Poodles who have been trained as tracking dogs. They can follow the path of a person who has gone ahead of them minutes or hours before and lead their owners to the location of the lost person or child. In Alaska, there is even a man who has a team of sled dogs made up entirely of Standard Poodles. The dogs live out of doors just as the traditional Huskies do and are trained to pull a sled loaded with equipment and the owner over the frozen terrain of the far North.

Aside from the major role of all Poodles as companions, there are two additional areas that have become traditional for them. The first is in the field of obedience.

As a sport, obedience competition is a perfect activity for Poodles of all three sizes. They learn quickly, love to perform, are agile and athletic, and get along well with other people and dogs. Each year thousands of Poodles compete in obedience trails for titles such as Companion Dog, Companion Dog Excellent, Utility Dog, Utility Dog Excellent, and Obedience Trial Champion.

Beginning at the Novice (CD) level, and working all the way up to the OTCh title, Poodles excel at performing the various levels of achievement offered by the American Kennel Club and the United Kennel Club. Regardless of the level, Poodles and their owners, once bitten by the obedience bug, look forward with great anticipation to weekends when they can get out to the trials with their friends and competitors.

The second role is playing the part of watch and/or guard dog.

The smaller-sized Poodles make excellent alarm dogs that bark loudly and incessantly at the slightest hint of trouble. Just let a stranger approach your home and the Toy or Miniature Poodle will hear the person long before you do and begin his warning bark. On the other hand, Standard Poodles as guards of home and property present a force to be reckoned with.

When we think of protection dogs, we usually think of the large working or herding breeds, such as German Shepherds, Dobermans, Rottweilers, and Great Danes. But a true dog person, wise in the ways of many breeds, will tell you that only a fool would challenge the authority of a good Standard Poodle when he's protecting his home and family. (Many years ago, I had a chocolate brown Standard that, on more than one occasion, broke through a glass window to stop a man who was prowling around my yard in a most

*Poodles are easy to train and enjoy performing, which makes them ideal candidates for obedience competition.*

suspicious manner!) Large enough to be noticed, courageous enough to stand his ground against the most intimidating stranger, and intelligent enough to sense the difference between a harmless visitor and a stranger with trouble on his mind, the Standard Poodle makes an excellent guard dog. And when put to the test, he proves himself to be a formidable protector in a fancy disguise!

One such dog is Griffin, a black Standard who lives with his family in Fort Myers, Florida. Dawn and Troy Phillips live in a lovely suburban home with their almost-two-year-old daughter, Aubrie. Griffin was about 18 months old when Aubrie was born. From the day Aubrie came home from the hospital, Griffin designated himself as her private guardian. Patient, tolerant, loving, and ever alert to Aubrie's safety, the big dog never lets the child out of his sight as long as she's awake.

When Aubrie and Griffin play together at home, Griffin patiently allows Aubrie to dress him in Dawn's shoes, dark glasses, or whatever else the child can get her hands on. Aubrie frequently cuddles up beside Griffin, often laying with him for hours on the floor, the sofa, or wherever they happen to be when

*Aubrie and black Standard Griffin are such good friends that Griffin doubles as a pillow for the little girl.*

*Another of Griffin's fast friends is Scooter, a black Labrador Retriever.*

the need to rest arises. The big dog is so gentle that he frequently finds Aubrie's little hands in his open mouth, yet he never presses his teeth into that tender skin.

Every day, Dawn dons her roller blades, puts Aubrie in her stroller and Griffin on his lead, and starts out on a brisk journey around their community. If a stranger approaches, Griffin places himself between the person and Aubrie. Then, looking back at Dawn, he awaits word that the approaching person is friendly. Dawn has no doubt that if Griffin ever felt Aubrie's safety was being threatened, the dog would act in an appropriate manner.

When Griffin was a puppy, Dawn took him to obedience training classes where he learned how to obey; basic commands such as sit, down, stay and come. Sometimes Griffin and Troy go for long walks together. When that happens, Dawn and Aubrie usually follow at a slower pace. Griffin will allow Troy to get no more than a half a block ahead of his little charge. Seeing that Dawn and Aubrie are falling too far behind for his

*Versatile, beautiful, intelligent, the Poodle is sure to remain a popular pet for centuries to come.*

comfort, Griffin refuses to proceed with Troy until the others catch up to them. He makes it very clear that he intends on keeping Aubrie always within his sight.

*A favorite bed cannot be priced to sell, as Quart makes clear.*

This scenario, the big Poodle and the small child, is no doubt repeated many times over around the world every day. Poodles of all sizes are dedicated to their families and Standard Poodles, despite their elegant appearance, are big enough to lend meaning to the word protector.

Finally, news from a friend in Florida raises my love of Poodles a whole notch higher. Linda Brown's black Standard, Delilah, recently gave birth to nine puppies. One of the puppies, a large black male, went to a couple in Mississippi. That's not particularly unusual, but the reason for these folks choosing a Standard Poodle is!

The lady wanted a handsome, intelligent companion dog that would not shed. Her husband wanted a retriever to train for duck hunting. The folks did their homework and discovered that a Standard Poodle would be the perfect choice. Now their new puppy will undoubtedly meet both of their needs. It's nice to see a dog living the lifestyle that surges within his genes.

From these examples of Poodles in today's world, it becomes obvious that they are extremely versatile. That one trait alone is probably the main reason why they have remained among the most popular breeds of dog for decades. And there's no reason to suspect that they will, in the next century, fall from favor among dog lovers around the world.

# SELECTING Your Poodle

If I were allowed just one sentence to offer as advice to the potential puppy buyer, it would be: Do your homework! Look through an encyclopedia of dog breeds to see which ones catch your eye. Investigate the background of the breed or breeds of your interest. Read all the material you can find related to those breeds. Most libraries have a good selection of books on dogs.

Go to dog shows in your area. Most shows are advertised in local newspapers, on television, and on the radio. Seek out the people exhibiting your breeds of interest and ask questions. Most of all, observe the dogs and how they react to the stress and excitement of crowds and other dogs. Do the dogs appear to be having fun, or do they seem anxious, nervous, or even aggressive toward other dogs and strangers?

Talk to local dog trainers, obedience instructors, and veterinarians, and, by all means, listen carefully to what they have to say. For example, a person may say that a particular breed "isn't the easiest to train" when what they really mean is "this breed is tough. It takes a firm handler to get and maintain control of this breed." They may comment that their breed isn't crazy about cold weather. This translates to "My dog loves the heat and refuses to go out during the winter." This means you could have housetraining problems when the weather turns cold.

*Have some safe chew toys, like Nylabones®, ready for your Poodle when you bring him home.*

Evaluate for yourself whether you and your loved ones are the right types of people to cope with this particular breed.

Veterinarians will be able to tell you what health problems they most often see in your breeds of interest. Some physical problems are

*Remember, beyond the cute appeal of the Toy Poodle is a dog who needs regular attention, grooming and a winter coat to be happy.*

easy to manage and cause the dog little or no suffering. Others are more serious, can cause a great deal of suffering, and are often lifethreatening.

Keep in mind that all the people I have mentioned have no financial interest in sharing information with you. Owners, dog show exhibitors, veterinarians, trainers, and instructors are not directly rewarded by giving you advice. You may ultimately seek their professional help, but initially they want only to communicate their findings with genuinely interested parties.

Next, talk to breeders. These are the people responsible for producing puppies representative of a particular breed of dog. If the puppies grow up not looking and acting like the breed they represent, the breeder's credibility is to be questioned.

Reputable breeders care very much about the puppies they produce. They are also proud of their dogs' progeny and want only to see their puppies get into good homes where the breed will flourish and serve as good public relations examples to the world.

Talking with breeders is usually not a one-way conversation. Most will gladly answer your questions, volunteer more information than you thought necessary, and show a great deal of interest in you and your reasons for wanting a dog of their breed.

In my years as a breeder, I have turned away more than one person as a potential puppy buyer. Whether I felt that the person was unable to care for the puppy properly or that the person and his family were just too unfit to own a dog, I never hesitated to be courteous yet firm in my suggestion for them to either consider a different breed or another type of pet altogether. Perhaps those suggestions didn't make me new friends, but at least I felt good knowing that I had saved one of my puppies from a regrettable fate. As a breeder, my allegiance to my breed had to come first.

Another excellent source of information is the owners of some of the breeder's puppies. A reputable breeder is more than happy to refer you to some of his puppy buyers and those buyers are always delighted to have you meet their dogs and share their feelings about their choice of pet.

Your investigation should include looking at photos of some of the dogs produced and shown by the breeder. You'll be able to get a good idea of size, color, and type from these pictures. Ask to see the pedigrees of the sire and dam of the puppies in question. The breeder will also introduce you to the dam of the litter and, if available, the sire as well.

Pedigrees are the history of bloodlines that, combined through generations of breeding, go into making up the dogs you see today. I always find it fascinating that often a puppy will develop into a carbon copy of a grandparent, so study the pedigrees and get familiar with the bloodlines.

You're getting closer to a decision about what breed of dog will best fit into your lifestyle and bring you joy as a companion. There are perfect people and homes for almost every breed of dog. It remains for you to decide what's just the right breed for you.

## BEFORE YOU BUY

Next, you need to locate the source of your potential new dog. Sometimes people purchase a dog from a breeder who lives many miles away. This entails a series of letters, phone calls, photos, and much discussion, not to mention that the seller should come highly recommended by someone you know and trust.

Before you are ready to purchase a dog, you have even more details to work out. Let's take a look at some of the additional decisions you'll have to make before you write that check.

What sex of dog you buy will be among your first considerations. Females are usually gentle and enjoy staying close to home. Males are usually larger than females with heavier bone structure and often denser coats.

Either sex can and should be neutered unless the dog is destined for the show ring and a career of reproduction. Spaying a female or neutering a male has many good results. It makes the dogs mellower, more content to be with the family and in the home, and easier to control. On the other hand, it does not take away from their protective instincts or ability to function.

Intact males are interested in females throughout the year. Intact females usually come in season twice a year for 21 days each season and need to be confined if you don't want them getting pregnant. They can also become finicky and irritable at

*Joey and Oodles are a great example of how the right dog in the right family is wonderful for all.*

those times, and are extremely interested in male dogs of any breed.

Breeding puppies should be left to the breeders. Contrary to popular belief, breeding puppies rarely generates large profits for the breeder. The cost of stud fees, maintaining a breeding female before, during, and after breeding, and raising a litter of puppies is extremely high—much higher than most people care to admit.

Worming and vaccinating the puppies before they go to new homes is costly as well. Worming and immunizing puppies against distemper, hepatitis, parainfluenza, parvovirus, and coronavirus before the puppies can be sold is mandatory in many states.

If an emergency such as the need for a Cesarean delivery arises, the expenses become astronomical. This does not take into account the risk to the mother's life or her future ability to produce puppies. In most cases, this cannot be predicted in advance.

## WHAT AGE OF DOG?

When people think of acquiring a new dog, they most often think of a puppy—a baby puppy. that's between 8 and 12 weeks of age. Although the dictionary defines a puppy as a young dog less than one year of age, I break that down even further.

I consider a puppy to be between the ages of 8 and 20 weeks of age. An adolescent is from 5 to 12 months of age, and an adult dog is over 1 year of age.

*If you get your dog as a puppy, you can mold it to your lifestyle and teach it good habits from the start.*

There are advantages and disadvantages to purchasing a dog in each of these categories. You need to know what they are before you can make a well-informed decision about the dog that's going to be a part of your family for many years.

A puppy is like raw clay. You begin with good quality material and mold him to suit your lifestyle and wishes. Because he hasn't lived long enough to develop bad habits, you can begin teaching him good habits right from the start.

*You may want to consider getting an older Poodle instead of a puppy. Older dogs have lots of love to give and have usually had some training.*

*Chewing is a necessary part of being a dog, and you'll have to supply chew devices to puppies and adults.*

It's fascinating to observe the growth and development of youngsters, whether humans or dogs. Seeing how they learn, mature, and discover the world around them can be extremely exciting and rewarding.

On the minus side, you will have to deal with puppy teething and chewing, housetraining, jumping on people and furniture, and sometimes excessive barking and digging. You should plan on crate training your puppy and being prepared to take him outdoors frequently until his urinary system is fully developed at about six months of age. This means getting up several times during the night and serving breakfast at 6 a.m. Little puppies need to be fed three times a day.

Because they're teething and often have aching gums, little puppies love to chew on soft things, especially your hands and ankles. If you have toddlers or tiny babies to think of, large-breed dogs can be a problem if they are in the same stages of development as the human babies.

Small breed puppies can be sat on by toddlers and sometimes injured in the process. Further, toddlers don't always understand your attempts to train the puppy and frequently undo whatever it is you're trying to accomplish. Think about all these things before you decide on the age of puppy you'll buy.

Adolescent dogs have the early housetraining behind them and are usually pretty reliable when it comes to not having accidents in the house. Though there are still some developmental stages to go through, the adolescent usually understands what "no" means. He chews less because his permanent front teeth are in, but he still faces the emergence of molars that often causes some serious chewing on hard items. If you realize this, you can provide hard bones for chewing and teach him not to use your coffee table legs as chew toys.

The adolescent is still young enough to form a bond with you if you make an effort. He is eager to participate in your lifestyle, yet he occasionally needs a reminder to use good manners. You'll be able to witness the transformation from gangly teenager with long spindly legs that seem to go in every direction at once to graceful adult. All these stages of development are exciting to observe and participate in.

Whether you choose a baby puppy or an adolescent, you should plan on taking the dog to an obedience class for some basic training. Not only will he learn good manners and simple commands, such as sit, stay, down, and come, but he will build that bond with you as his master. This is the foundation from which all you do together for the rest of his life will come. It's worth the time and effort.

Now let's consider purchasing an adult dog. First, you need to know that adults for sale are rare compared to the availability of puppies. Occasionally you may see an advertisement in a newspaper for an adult, but you must seriously question the reasons why this dog is for sale. Sometimes people sell adults because of behavior problems that you will not be able to correct. In this case, you'll be stuck with someone else's problem.

Once in a while a reputable breeder will offer to sell an adult because the dog's show career has ended, possibly because of age or physical problems. The breeder will usually spay or neuter the dog and look for a good pet home for him.

With an adult dog, there are no growing-up problems to face, but you must be prepared to allow the dog enough time to adjust to his new home with you. This requires a lot of patience on your part, but it can be most rewarding.

Adult dogs are ideal purchases for older people with limited physical abilities and stamina. Providing the dog is well-mannered, the adult dog can better fit into a quieter, slower lifestyle than a young puppy.

A young family with active children does not make an ideal home for an older dog if the dog has had no prior experiences with growing children and all that implies. If, however, an adult

*Taking your puppy or adult Poodle to obedience classes will help him learn the basic commands, such as sit and down.*

dog is coming from an active family that included young children, the dog will likely learn to love his new young masters and fit in well. It will be up to you to determine whether or not your home situation is similar to that from which the adult is coming.

The cost of an adult dog is often much less than it is for a puppy or adolescent. The purpose in placing an adult dog is usually for the best interest of the dog, so price is rarely a consideration. The bottom line for the breeder is whether or not the adult dog will fit well into your home and family unit.

*When selecting a pup, look at the whole litter if possible and ask the breeder questions so you pick the pup best suited to you.*

## SOCIALIZATION

Regardless of the age of dog you choose to purchase, one of the most important factors in choosing a new dog is how you perceive that dog when you first meet him and spend some time getting to know him. We've all heard the story about the person who was searching for a dog, found one, and upon meeting the animal, discovered that he and the dog were made for each other.

However, a dog of any age, even a puppy, that runs from you, hides in a corner, or in any way acts frightened of your presence is not an ideal candidate no matter how appealing he may look. The key, therefore, to preventing this problem of the dog's shyness in the first place is socialization. And socialization must begin with the breeder long before you ever meet the dog.

As a matter of fact, the older a dog is before socialization begins, the more difficult it is for the dog to adjust to new situations and surroundings. Some dogs, deprived of early socialization, are never able to adjust to new homes and people and are therefore doomed to live out their lives in their original homes never knowing how wonderful and full life can be.

Socializing a puppy beginning when he is four or five weeks of age starts with letting family members and friends hold and play

*The more places you take your dog to and the more people you introduce him to—especially children—-the better your dog will be able to handle changes.*

with him. He should be subjected to a wide variety of situations and environments such as a backyard, a kitchen, a park, a ride in the car just for fun, and a visit to meet children and other pets. In other words, the young puppy should be exposed to a cross-section of life as he will know it when he becomes an adult.

Once the puppy is settled in his new home, the same procedure must be repeated regularly in new surroundings with all new people and pets. If this socialization is approached on a basis of fun and with the reward of positive attention, the puppy's confidence level will grow so he can cope with life and all it has to offer.

That's one of the major advantages to puppy kindergarten and beginner's training classes. The exposure to new dogs, people, and experiences assures a well-balanced adult dog that is sure of himself and his family.

If you're considering an adolescent, make sure that he has been properly and adequately socialized during his formative months (between two and five months of age). You can tell if this is so by observing how he handles meeting you and your family.

So look for the dog, either puppy or adult, that accepts you and appears interested in interacting with you. Needless to say, an adult that shows signs of lacking socialization should not be considered for purchase. A full-grown Standard Poodle, for example, is a large dog, and a fearful one may be prone to fear biting. A frightened Toy, small as he is, can still do major damage if he resorts to biting. Regardless of the reason for biting, a bite is a bite and must be considered a serious matter.

I have known a number of people who have taken non-socialized dogs into their homes because they felt sorry for them. They wanted to work with the dogs and give them a good life.

*A well-socialized dog will be able to get along comfortably with other animals and people.*

This, however, was never accomplished and frequently ended when the dog either ran away or bit someone and was euthanized as a final solution. In all those cases, the people involved were heartbroken when they realized they could not change behavioral patterns that had been formed in the developmental stages of the dog's life.

In short, socialization or the lack of it serves to

determine the path a dog's behavior will follow for his entire life. That being the case, which incidentally has been proven by scientific studies, socialization affects you as much as the dog.

## REGISTRATION

At this point, let's address the matter of kennel clubs, registrations, pedigrees, and what they mean to you. Kennel clubs are registering bodies for purebred dogs. In addition, they maintain records of things such as championship titles, sporting event degrees, and offspring produced by individual dogs registered with them.

For example, when an American Kennel Club registered sire (father) and dam (mother) produce a litter of puppies, the breeder registers the litter's birth with the AKC. Each puppy in that litter is then given an individual registration application form that goes with the puppy to the new owner.

In a recent public information ad, the American Kennel Club wrote, "If you buy a purebred dog that you are told is eligible for registration with the American Kennel Club, you are entitled to receive from the seller an application form that will enable you to register your dog.

*These six-week-old pups have a few weeks to go before they leave home. Make sure the breeder gives you your puppy's registration application.*

*Breeders hold off on naming puppies so that new owners can give the dogs the name they've selected.*

"If the seller cannot give you the application, you should demand and receive full identification of your dog in writing, signed by the seller, consisting of the breed, the registered names and individual registration numbers of your dog's sire and dam, your dog's date of birth, the name of its breeder and, if available, its AKC litter number.

"Don't be misled by promises of 'papers' later."

The new owner selects a name for his puppy and registers that name with the AKC, which, in turn, gives the puppy his own individual registration number. That number stays with the dog for life. The number is also used to trace the ancestors of the dog and create a pedigree, or genealogical record. The pedigree will tell you the names of a given dog's parents, grandparents, great-grandparents, etc.

If you purchase a puppy whose sire and dam are not known, but you believe it to be a purebred, you may apply to the AKC for an Indefinite Listing Privilege number. An Indefinite Listing Privilege (ILP) number allows you to exhibit the dog in AKC sporting events and earn titles. A dog with an ILP may not, however, be exhibited in the conformation ring or earn a breed championship title.

To obtain an ILP number, write to the AKC for an application form. They will probably ask for pictures of your dog and written statements from knowledgeable experts who testify that, in their opinions, your dog is a purebred.

If, after investigating your claim, the AKC agrees that your dog is a purebred, they will issue a number and send you a certificate to that effect. From then on you may participate in AKC dog activities for fun.

When choosing a puppy, take a hard look first at the home or kennel. Is the atmosphere chaotic or orderly? Do the adult dogs appear friendly and healthy? Does the breeder appear knowledgeable about his or her breed? Is he or she concerned about the welfare of the puppies and their future homes?

Next, look at the whole litter and their living quarters. Their sleeping and play areas should be clean and free of unpleasant odors. If the puppies are using newspaper for elimination, it should be changed as needed. If they're outdoors, their elimination area should show signs of frequent clean-up.

If possible, observe the puppies eating a meal and see how they react to each other. Look for puppies that eat eagerly and do not act aggressively toward littermates. Overprotectiveness of food at this early age may signal problems in the adult dog.

Do the puppies appear active and healthy? They should have bright eyes with no discharge coming from them. Their stools should be well-formed with no signs of diarrhea. Their coats

*Notice everything about the place from which you buy your dog, including the cleanliness of the grounds.*

should be fluffy and full and should be clean and free of parasites such as fleas and ticks.

As your eyes begin to focus on certain puppies in the litter, concentrate on their behavior, because it often predicts what they will be like as adults. For example, the bully of the litter may grow up to become a very dominant individual that is sometimes difficult to control. The runt, or smallest one, may not fit your criteria for a busy lifestyle, as he may grow up to be very timid or he may develop in the opposite direction and become the tyrant of the neighborhood.

*The friendly Poodle gets along well with other people and pets.*

A friendly, outgoing, yet not hyperactive, puppy begins life with a lot going for him. He should be curious and alert, have a bright intelligence in his expression, and be eager to hang around people.

Among dog folk there is an old saying that there are basically two kinds of dog: dog dogs and people dogs. The dog dogs are happiest when they're with their own kind and will spend their lives attempting to socialize with other dogs. Human companionship is secondary to them.

People dogs are more content to be with you. They accept other dogs, but prefer the company of their owners and will almost always choose you over other pets. This is the type of dog that will be eager to learn, anxious to please, and happy doing things with you all his life.

If you're interested in exhibiting in the breed ring, not only must you consider temperament but you must look at the puppy and consider what he'll look like as an adult. Here's where the help of the breeder is paramount. Nobody can accurately predict how a puppy will turn out, but the breeder, particularly if he has a history

*Keep in mind that a show-quality dog is going to be more expensive than a pet-quality dog, but you will receive the same amount of love from each of them.*

of raising good quality show dogs, is in a position to assist you in making the best choice. For example, the breeder will have a good idea of the puppy's eventual size, coat color, and type.

The price of a show puppy will probably be much more than the price of a puppy destined for a pet home. After all, the show dog will be shown at a great cost in time, training, and money and will ultimately be bred to contribute more fine specimens to the breed in years to come. For example, if and when your puppy grows up to become a champion, the price you can demand for the stud fee of a male or the puppies of a female will be much higher than the price for puppies from pet stock.

On the other hand, you can purchase a pet-quality puppy out of the same litter from which a show, quality puppy comes. The difference in show and pet quality is often very small and noticeable only to trained experts. The pet puppy, however, has come from the same parents, has had the same quality upbringing, and has received the same socialization and start in life that his show-quality littermate has had. The fact that the show puppy may have the potential for a thicker coat, a longer muzzle, or heavier bone as an adult will not affect the pet-quality puppy or you. You will be benefiting from the care and attention the entire litter received before, during, and after birth.

In addition, you will still be able to train and exhibit your dog in obedience trials and earn titles for your dog. The sport of obedience is exciting and rewarding and is open to all purebred dogs regardless of whether or not they are show quality or sexually altered.

In fact, when you review the puppy's pedigree, you may see dogs listed with CD, CDX, UD, or UDX following their names. These obedience titles are significant in demonstrating the willingness and capability of those individuals to work with their owners. To document this, the dogs have been exhibited at obedience trials, thereby proving their value as companion animals.

The initials TD and TDX after a dog's name indicate that the dog has earned an AKC Tracking Dog or Tracking Dog Excellent title. Tracking is teaching a dog to use his nose to follow the path of someone who has gone ahead of him minutes or hours before. Whether Toy, Miniature, or Standard, the dog has established himself as a hearty individual who has proved his worth for more things than just fun and entertainment.

If you're purchasing a puppy from a local hobby breeder who has bred a litter of puppies for the first time, you need to be particularly careful in your selection. First, the mother of the litter has no record of what she produces in size, coat color, temperament, etc. Ask the owner where the dam came from—that information could be a clue as to what you can expect from her puppies.

*Even if you don't plan to show your Poodle, he will greatly benefit from basic training.*

If the female was bred to a local pet male, you may

want to visit his home and meet him. Study his behavior and observe his appearance and general physical condition as well as his disposition. If you don't like the parents, don't buy the puppy.

Perhaps if you do your homework now, you may be as fortunate as I was many years ago when I purchased a female Miniature Schnauzer named Brandy from a first time hobby breeder. Brandy's dam had been bred to a champion and the owner of the female was being guided in her breeding program by reputable breeders with years of experience.

Brandy ultimately grew up to be a fine specimen of the breed with a correct temperament. When she was two years old, I bred her to a champion and she produced four puppies. Two of them became champions and the start of a long line of well-known Miniature Schnauzers.

Now let's focus our attention on puppy coats and colors. Unlike many breeds of dog that are born with the exact same color as their parents, Poodles are not. Depending on the eventual color that the Poodle will be, puppies can be born a dark brown, black, even a rich cream. As the puppy matures, the color will change until he finally develops the coat that will be his for life.

Black Poodles are born black. Gray ones, however, are born black and gradually change to gray or blue as they mature. It isn't at all unusual to see a black puppy with a gray face, for the face is usually the first part of the body to change.

Poodles of the brown phases, such as cafe-au-lait and chocolate, have livered-colored noses, eye-rims, and lips. Those in the black, blue, gray, silver, cream, and white phases have black noses, eye-rims, and lips.

Rich caramel and brown puppies may change to light cream and apricot tan as adults. Sometimes a cream female will produce almost-white puppies with tan-colored feathering on the tips of the ears. As they grow, the coat color will darken a bit and the ear color will lighten, producing soft, pale cream adults similar to their parents.

The texture of the Poodle coat also changes with maturity. Born with soft, straight, fluffy fur, the puppy's coat changes to the desired double coat of wiry curls mixed with softer undercoat. It can take about a year for some Poodles to change to their adult color and coat texture, while some Standards take even longer than that.

If possible, investigate the health of both parents of the puppy you're considering. In particular, you will want to know whether or not either parent has a hereditary physical problem.

## Specific Health Problems of the Poodle

Just as human beings experience certain physical illnesses and conditions, so, too, do dogs of all breeds. As such, some breeds have a higher incidence of certain conditions than others. Within the Poodle breed, there are some conditions that are hereditary and others that are not.

Cruciate ligament injury happens when one of the two criss-crossed ligaments in the knee is ruptured. Overweight

*The color and texture of your Poodle's coat will change as he gets older. This pup will lighten and develop a true double coat.*

dogs are more prone to this condition than dogs at a perfect weight. Surgical treatment for the torn ligament usually restores the dog's ability to use the leg as well as stops related pain.

Knee joint dislocation is another condition that usually requires surgery and may even be hereditary in some bloodlines of Poodles.

Two eye problems are seen in Poodles: cataracts and progressive retinal atrophy. Both can be hereditary and both can cause blindness. The inherited type of cataract, also known as juvenile cataracts, can occur at any age. Cataracts seen in older dogs are frequently observed in diabetic individuals.

Swallowing foreign objects is a common habit of puppies and Poodles are no exception. If the object is small enough, it may pass through the GI system harmlessly. If not, it can cause a blockage of the intestines that sometimes requires surgery to remove. If the blockage problem is ignored, the

*Poodles are known to suffer from cataracts and progressive retinal atrophy. Ask if your dog's bloodlines are affected.*

*When it's right, you know it. This is Honey Loring and Olympia—a match made in heaven.*

condition may prove fatal. Supervising puppies and what they put in their mouths is the obvious answer to the problem of foreign matter ingestion. Like small children, puppies are curious and seem to have a need to taste and/or chew anything they can get into their mouths.

The decision to bring a dog into your home and life is not a decision to be rushed into. The best choice for you to make is an informed, intelligent one. I said it before, and I will say it again. For the best chance at getting a Poodle that will become a great companion, *do your homework.*

# CARING for Your Poodle

The big day is about to arrive. You've done your homework, you've been to dog shows and talked to a lot of people about a lot of dogs, you've decided that a Poodle, either a Toy, a Miniature, or a Standard, is the best breed for you, and you've found just the right puppy that makes your heart beat faster. What next?

Before you introduce the new member of your family into your home, let's go over some of the things you'll need to think about and have ready before you actually get the puppy. If you make appropriate arrangements beforehand, you and the puppy will experience a smooth transition from birth environment to new home. The big day, and even the weeks to come, will be smooth and pleasant for all concerned.

## FEEDING

Talk to the breeder and get a list of the kinds and brands of food the puppy has been fed. Dogs have very sensitive digestive systems, so changing brands abruptly will usually cause diarrhea and great discomfort to the puppy, to say nothing of the extra clean-up work for you.

*Suddenly changing your puppy's diet could cause him stress and stomach upset. Follow the breeder's diet for as long as possible and make any changes gradually.*

Also record the number of meals per day that the puppy has been eating and the times of day he's eaten. Try to maintain this schedule for at least two weeks after you get him. Changing his environment and being separated from his dam and siblings is traumatizing enough—he does not need physical stress added to this.

Water should also be available at all times during the day when he's out of his crate. At night, however, it's wise to restrict water

*Your Poodle should eat a quality commercial dog food to supply him with the nutrients he needs.*

consumption to a few sips after the last meal of the day. You and the puppy will not want to get up too many times during the night.

Never feed a puppy from your plate or the dinner table. It may be cute when he's a tiny baby, but cute turns to nuisance when he becomes an adult. Right from day one he needs to know that his meals come from his bowl, not yours.

Dogs should eat dog food, not junk food. The major dog food manufacturers spend millions of dollars a year on researching the best diets for canines. Make use of this information and avoid feeding your puppy foods that will not help him grow properly or that may cause stomach upset.

If and when you want to switch brands and/or types of dog food, talk to your veterinarian. He will suggest an appropriate diet and the amount of food and number of meals per day that will most benefit your puppy.

As a general rule, puppies between two and six months of age should be served three meals a day. From 6 to 12 months, puppies should be given 2 meals a day. When the puppy reaches one year of age, you may feed him once or twice a day for life.

I prefer to feed my adults twice a day. That way, I can feed smaller amounts, which will not cause stomach bloating, and the dogs seem to enjoy eating at the same times as my family does. After all, smelling food cooking in the kitchen stimulates their appetites as well as ours, so twice daily works for us.

Always feed your puppy in the same place and never allow children to bother the puppy while he's eating. I choose to feed my dogs in the kitchen. It's clean, near the area of preparation, free of insects that are attracted to food outdoors, and it allows me an opportunity to observe how eagerly and how much each dog consumes.

Free feeding is an option whereby you place dry food in a bowl and just let the puppy help himself whenever the mood strikes. This method, however, has several disadvantages.

First, you'll never know exactly how much and when a puppy is eating. Second, food left out can spoil quickly in warm temperatures and make your dog sick. And third, you miss seeing any subtle hints that the puppy is not feeling well when he nibbles half-heartedly.

By feeding on a regular schedule where you can observe the puppy eating, you're able to monitor the puppy's general health and exactly how he's feeling at any given time. Thus, when problems occur, this method draws your attention to the onset of trouble before it becomes serious.

When feeding puppies and adults, put down the food bowl and leave it alone for 15 minutes. At the end of that time, remove the bowl and offer no more food until the next scheduled meal. Dogs quickly figure out that when the food bowl is presented, they'd better get right to it before you take it away. No chance for attracting unwanted pests in the kitchen or for developing picky eaters this way.

## EXERCISE

Exercise is another critical matter to consider. There are several kinds of exercises we need to address. Exercising for elimination, for muscle building and coordination skills, for fun and bonding, and for learning are all important aspects of helping your puppy grow.

Elimination exercising should be limited to specific areas so that your command "let's go out" (or whatever phrase you care to use) plus going to the same area each time will help your puppy associate eliminating with your command. Taking him for long walks through the neighborhood is not the way to teach housetraining as the puppy has so much to investigate that eliminating becomes lost in the adventure of exploring the neighborhood. Then, when he gets back in the house, he suddenly remembers that he has to go and another accident happens.

Once the puppy is housetrained, he can be offered opportunities to discover his neighborhood. By then his body will also be strong enough to benefit from extended exercising.

*Your Poodle needs a sufficient amount of daily exercise to maintain the proper health and a good physical condition.*

*Having your child take part in caring for the family pet is a good lesson in responsibility. It also helps a child feel comfortable around animals.*

For the 8-week-old puppy, just following you around the kitchen and family room will soon tire him out and he'll collapse into a deep sleep for anywhere from 10 to 30 minutes. As the puppy grows, his capacity for exercise will increase and you'll see his need for more and more exercise grow with him.

If there are young children in the family, don't allow them to overdo play and exercise with the puppy. You should always be there to supervise any interaction between the children and the dog. Teaching children how to treat the puppy and teaching the puppy how to act with children is all part of your responsibility when raising them both.

One trick I developed years ago with children was to teach the "sit and hold" habit. Rather than let little children hold puppies while standing up, I taught the kids to sit on the floor when they wanted to hold a puppy. That way, if the puppy wriggled out of their arms, the puppy wouldn't have far to fall, thus preventing potentially serious accidents.

Taking the puppy to different environments such as a shopping center, park, beach, or a wooded trail not only serves to socialize the puppy but gives him plenty of exercise to strengthen his developing muscles. In addition, it serves to help you and the puppy build a strong bond of loyalty to each other.

Finally, exercising as a form of learning brings great pleasure to both teacher (you) and student (puppy). Playing hide-and-seek in the house or a fenced backyard is good exercise for the puppy while he learns to come to you for praise and a treat.

*The author and Ginger enjoy a leisurely bike ride in the sun and fresh air.*

Because most Poodles are natural retrievers, teaching fetch is fun and easy. Use a soft toy such as one of the Nylabone® chew toys. Interest the puppy in getting it by wiggling it on the floor in front of him. When his interest is keen, toss it a few feet away as you say "get it." When he runs out to pick it up, say "Good boy. Bring it here." It won't be long before he gets the idea that if he brings it back to you, you'll toss it again. Always praise him lavishly when he picks up and carries the toy.

To assure complete and proper bone development, don't allow puppies under one year of age to jump. However, any other active game can encourage muscle development and be fun for the puppy. Just keep the games short and lively.

Toys are an important part of puppy development for several reasons. First, every infant, whether human or animal, needs to learn to play because play is really practice for handling life situations in adulthood.

Play fighting, play hunting, play mating, play stalking, play grooming, and power playing are nature's way of teaching the young puppy how to conduct himself when he grows up. It provides practical lessons in how to interact with his own kind and succeed.

Play also provides an opportunity for muscle development. Running, chasing, catching, climbing, and similar type activities serve to strengthen growing bodies.

Second, playing with you is extremely beneficial to the bond that you and the dog build together. Playing reinforces the idea that he is most certainly a vital member of your pack.

*The Poodle will thrive with an owner who leads an active lifestyle and devotes time and attention to his pet.*

*Having fun with your dog definitely strengthens the bond between you.*

When you control the games, begin and end the games at your discretion, not the puppy's. It sends a message to the puppy that you are the pack leader. That in itself teaches him to respect you, and makes his learning other behaviors more meaningful.

Finally, playing with other people is important, too. He learns to play gently with children and older folks. He learns to inhibit his bite reflex and use his mouth in a gentle manner. He learns body control and how to use his energy efficiently. He learns self-control and all about the rewards it brings through attention and affection.

We see then that toys and playing are paramount to raising a well-rounded individual with good physical and mental skills that will serve him well for life.

# GROOMING Your Poodle

All dogs need to be groomed regularly, and Poodles more so than most. Because Poodles don't shed their coats, their hair must be cut. Because styles vary depending on whether the Poodle is a show dog or pet, the actual grooming can be relatively simple or rather extensive. Fortunately, pet owners have some choices in how and when their dogs are groomed.

Professional groomers can take a dog and sculpt an elegant style or clip the coat into a utilitarian cut. The professional will also brush out the coat, bathe the dog, and then scissor the remainder of the body to your desired style. Prices for professional grooming depend on the amount of work needed to produce the look you desire. Prices also depend on the size of the Poodle being groomed. Removing the hair from the inner ears and trimming the toenails are included in the charge and part of the regular regimen of grooming. Some professional groomers also polish the toenails and add a bow to the pet's topknot as a final touch. Regular grooming should be performed about every six to eight weeks providing the owner bathes and brushes the coat

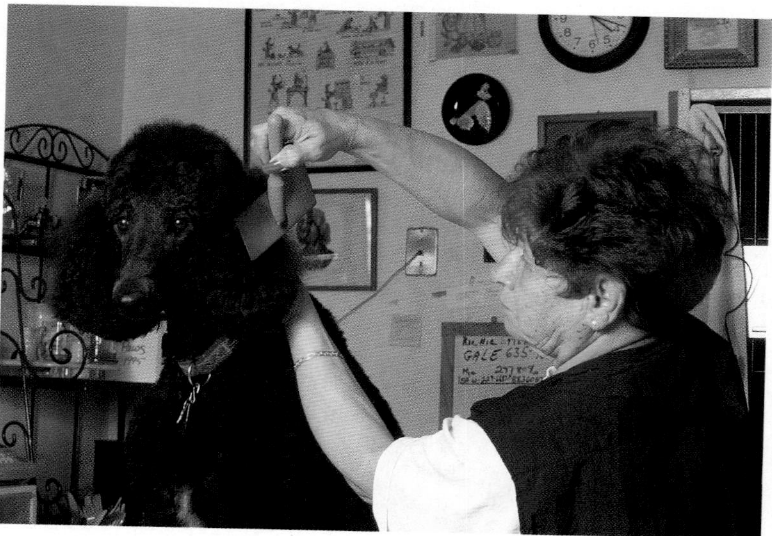

*Even though your Poodle doesn't shed, she still needs regular grooming to keep her coat clean and tangle-free.*

regularly at home between groomings.

If you wish to learn how to groom your own Poodle, there are courses you can take as well as some professionals who will, for a fee, teach you how to do it yourself. I have always groomed all my Poodles and I enjoy the time spent in doing so.

*Regular grooming sessions combined with an all-over body check will help you to stay on top of your dog's physical condition.*

Routinely, I brush my Poodles twice a week, bathe them once a week, and trim their nails about every ten days. I shave their faces, feet, and bases of tails every six weeks as well as scissor their bodies, topknots, and legs at that time. This way, they always look nice and their coats are free of knots.

Ideally, your new puppy should come to you having been groomed at least once by the breeder. The face, feet, and base of tail will have been shaved, the coat bathed and brushed out thoroughly, the nails trimmed if necessary, and the inside of the ears cleaned and free of hair.

These first experiences must begin early in the Poodle's life. Let's face it, a groomable breed needs to learn as a tiny puppy that grooming is simply a basic part of life and he must accept the process with tolerance and grace.

Keeping the Poodle's coat free from foreign matter and those dreaded knots is really quite easy. The secret to maintaining a good coat is frequency of brushing. Like the dog itself, the Poodle owner must accept the fact that regular brushing is simply a part of Poodle ownership. While the puppy is growing, brushing daily not only keeps the coat clean but also serves to train the puppy to accept grooming without resistance. Once the puppy reaches maturity, you can reduce the daily brushing to three or four times a week and still maintain a good coat. What's more, if properly trained, the Poodle will learn to love grooming time because the results make him feel good and he enjoys your attention.

I have divided the process into four specific steps: brushing, bathing, clipping, and scissoring. You may choose to have a professional groom your dog regularly while you maintain the coat in between groomings. That would include bathing and brushing.

If you want to groom the dog yourself, then you will need to learn how to perform each of the four steps in order to have a Poodle that always looks nice and has healthy skin and a healthy coat. You can learn ear cleaning and nail trimming from a professional groomer or your veterinarian.

### BRUSHING

Equipment needed will be a stiff wire brush commonly referred to as a slicker brush. A metal dog comb is also helpful in removing burrs and stickers before they develop into huge matted areas that require cutting out later.

Brushing the Poodle coat is called line brushing and is the best method for keeping the dog knot-free. Begin at the tail end of the dog and brush toward the head. With one hand, take up a section of hair. With the slicker brush in the other hand, draw the hair out of the hand starting from the root end of the hair and moving toward the tip of the hair.

When all of the hair has been brushed out of your hand, take the next section of hair and repeat the process. Brush gently and slowly and do not allow the bristles to scrape the dog's skin.

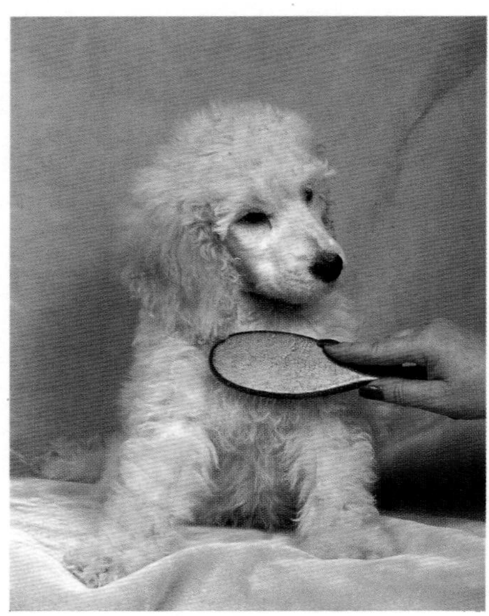

*It's a good idea to acclimate your Poodle to grooming procedures as soon as possible.*

*Show Poodles need extra-special grooming. These two have wraps and rubber bands in their coats to keep them clean and manageable.*

As you work, you'll notice that as the brush pulls the hair from your hand it creates a line of exposed flesh between the brushed and not-brushed hair. That's why they call it line brushing. If you don't see a line of skin, you'll know that you're brushing too much hair at one time and not getting the brush through every strand of hair.

Remember that brushing great chunks of hair at a time only covers the outer layer, leaving the hairs underneath unbrushed and probably filled with tiny knots. It's those tiny knots that can grow into huge mats, causing the dog severe discomfort and possible skin problems beneath them.

Work your way forward until you've brushed out the entire body, topknot, and ears. Then brush each leg and the tail. As you do, you'll notice how fluffy the coat becomes and how much nicer the dog looks.

*This show dog knows what's next: a thorough combing through before setting every hair in place.*

Always brush the coat before bathing the dog. If you reverse the process, the knots in the coat will become even worse when they get wet. Actually, that means you'll have to brush the dog twice, once before bathing and again after he's dry. However, the second brushing will be quick and easy.

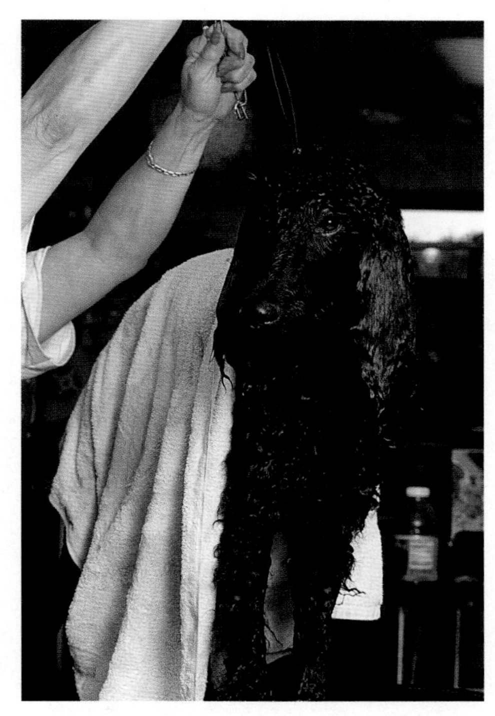

*Help your Poodle enjoy bath time by praising and rewarding him with treats.*

With proper and patient training from you, cooperation from the dog, and experience in handling the coat and the brush simultaneously, you'll find that you can brush out a Miniature Poodle in a mere few minutes. Standards take longer due to their size, but you can always divide the brushing process into two sessions with a pleasant break in between.

## Bathing

When bathing the Poodle, make it fun for the dog and he'll soon learn to love bath time. Whenever I begin raising a Poodle puppy, I teach the dog that bath time is fun and always followed by a special treat such as a biscuit or a piece of cheese. My adult Poodles come running from wherever they are when they hear me say "It's bath time!"

Use a regular dog shampoo and warm water when you bathe your Poodle. Wet the dog down, apply shampoo and rub it into a lather the same way you shampoo your own hair. Rinse thoroughly with warm water and follow that with a brisk towel drying.

The final drying can be left to nature providing you keep the dog out of extremely cold air and drafts until he's completely dry. If you let him dry naturally, you'll notice that his hair will dry in little ringlets all over his body. The final brushing will smooth out those ringlets somewhat, but if you want a really fluffy look to his coat, you'll need to use a hair dryer set on medium or low and brush the coat as it dries.

With this method, the hair will dry longer and straighter, thus giving the dog a fuller, fluffier look. Proceed slowly over the body, legs, topknot, and tail until the dog is completely dry. The final scissoring to sculpt the body, legs, and topknot will follow the drying. Sculpting hair that has been blow-dried is easier and more successful than trying to sculpt hair that has dried naturally.

If your dog gets paint or tar-type substances on his coat, apply a liberal amount of mineral oil to the substance, let it soak in for ten minutes, then rub briskly with an absorbent cloth. Follow with a good bath. Stronger chemicals used to remove paint can cause burning and irritation to the skin that may require subsequent veterinary attention and great suffering to the dog.

*Regularly brushing your Poodle's coat will keep it looking lustrous and neat.*

## CLIPPING AND SCISSORING

Equipment needed is as follows: a quality electric clipper, a minimum of two clipper blades (#10 and #15), several different types of scissors (such as short hair trimming shears), curved scissors for sculpting, and a pair of large shears for the dense, heavy body coat. A Poodle comb and a mat splitter will also come in handy. A pair of hemostats will be used to pull ear hair. Finally, a pair of nail clippers and a nail file for smoothing rough nails, plus some styptic powder to stop bleeding if you should cut a nail too short, are also necessary.

*Maintaining a positive and gentle attitude when grooming your Poodle will help make him more comfortable and cooperative.*

At the least, clipping and scissoring are utilitarian; at the most, they're forms of art. Each Poodle owner must decide for himself what route to take in keeping the dog well-groomed. Having a professional groomer do the job every six to eight weeks assures that the dog will have a trained expert set and maintain the pattern and style chosen by the owner. Keep in mind that the cost of such service must be included in your monthly budget.

Choosing to do it yourself means that you'll need some instruction, time, patience, and experience to get the job done. Unlike the professional who grooms many dogs every day, you will have to wait six to eight weeks between each grooming to build up experience to a point where you feel comfortable grooming your dog.

Although you'll save the cost of professional grooming, you'll need to plan on spending a sizable sum initially to purchase the equipment needed. Then you'll need some instruction and no matter what method you choose, it, too, will cost money.

There are several excellent books on the market offering complete instructions for grooming Poodles. Purchasing a video can be very helpful because you'll actually see how a professional does it. Taking lessons from a dog grooming school or a professional willing to instruct you privately will also be an initial expense. The one good thing about taking private lessons from a groomer is that you can usually use your own Poodle as the subject. That way, both you and your dog can become accustomed to working together at the grooming table. In addition, the groomer may point out certain features about your particular Poodle and teach you certain grooming tips to enhance your dog's appearance.

Unfortunately, clipping and scissoring instructions cannot be given in this book as the process requires an entire volume to cover adequately. Suffice it to say that there seems to be two very distinct mindsets among Poodle owners. One says, "I don't

*It might take a lot of work to get a Poodle looking as pretty as a picture, but for most owners, it's worth it.*

mind paying for professional grooming because I just don't have the time or interest in it myself." The other says, "I love grooming my Poodle and look forward to each grooming session with my dog."

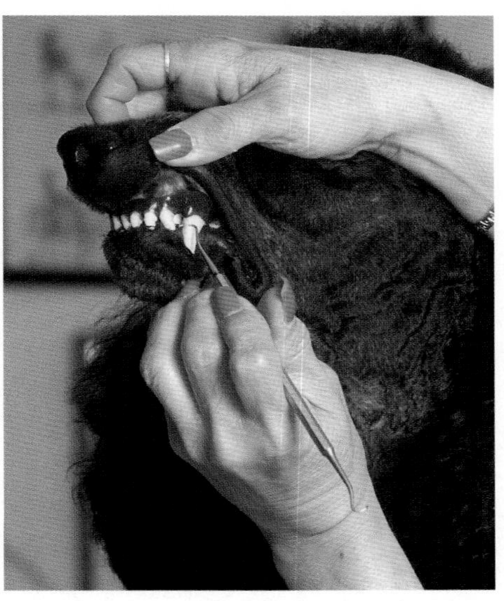

*Providing your Poodle with the proper dental care will help increase the longevity of his life.*

There is a middle-of-the-road approach, however. Many Poodle owners choose to have a professional groom the dog every six to eight weeks and they, the owners, maintain the coat in between grooming times. Whatever you decide, be assured that Poodles should not be considered if you have no intention of keeping the dog well groomed. For Poodles, coat care is a necessity—you have no other choice.

## Other Grooming Matters

I must mention that dental care is essential for a healthy mouth. Your veterinarian can teach you how to clean your dog's teeth. He'll also suggest the best products for oral hygiene.

Toenails must be trimmed regularly. If you begin trimming toenails when the puppy is young and teach him to sit still for trimming, you'll have no problem when he becomes an adult. However, waiting until the dog is full-grown and having him hate nail trimming can be dangerous. By then, he may attempt to bite the trimmer. This is unacceptable behavior.

At this point, the veterinarian will have to muzzle the dog for trimming and you'll have to pay extra for it. So make it economical for yourself and easy on the dog—teach nail trimming from an early age.

Having a well-groomed Poodle usually indicates a healthy Poodle and a caring owner who takes great pride in his friend.

# HOUSETRAINING and Training

A few general comments here seem in order before we get into the mechanics of housetraining. First of all, Poodles are very easy to housetrain, usually getting the idea of where they are to eliminate within a matter of several days. Some seem to know even before they leave their littermates.

Teaching a Poodle to use an indoor facility, such as a laundry room or bathroom, is entirely realistic for the Toy Poodle, manageable for the Miniature Poodle, and impossible for the Standard. When you think about the amount of stool produced by the dog when he becomes an adult, you'll realize that Standards must be trained to relieve themselves outdoors.

I train all my dogs, regardless of size, to relieve themselves outdoors even in bad weather. Picking up stool from the lawn or curb does not bother me, but patrolling the laundry room for dirty newspapers is just too unpleasant.

*If you take your Poodle to the same place to eliminate every time, he'll know what is expected of him.*

Success that comes by luck is usually a happenstance and frequently short-lived. Success that comes by well-thought-out, proven methods is often more easily achieved and permanent. This Success Method is designed to give you, the puppy owner, a simple yet proven way to help your puppy develop clean living habits and a feeling of security in his new environment.

## TYPES OF TRAINING

You can train a puppy to relieve himself wherever you choose. For example, city dwellers often train their puppies to relieve themselves in the gutter because large

*In the early stages of housetraining, it helps to accompany your puppy and praise when he performs the desired behavior.*

plots of grass are not readily available. Suburbanites, on the other hand, usually have yards to accommodate their dogs' needs.

Outdoor training includes such surfaces as grass, dirt, and cement. Indoor training usually means training a dog to eliminate on newspaper or in a paper-lined litter pan (appropriate for Miniature and Toy Poodles).

When deciding on the surface and location that you'll want your dog to use, be sure it's going to be permanent. Training a dog to grass and then changing your mind two months later is extremely difficult for both dog and owner.

Next, choose the command you'll use each and every time you want your puppy to void. "Go hurry up" and "Go make" are examples of commands commonly used by dog owners.

Get in the habit of asking the puppy, "Do you want to go hurry up?" (or whatever your chosen relief command is) before you take him out. That way, when he becomes an adult, you'll be able to determine if he wants to go out when you ask him. A confirmation will be signs of interest, wagging his tail, watching you intently, going to the door, etc.

Most of all, be consistent. Always take your dog to the same location, always use the same command, and always have him lead when he's in his relief area.

By following the Success Method, your puppy will be completely housetrained by the time his muscle and brain development reach maturity. Keep in mind that small breeds usually mature faster than large breeds, but all puppies should be trained by six months of age.

## PUPPY'S NEEDS

A puppy needs to relieve himself after play periods, after each meal, after he's been sleeping, and any time he indicates he's looking for a place to urinate or defecate.

The urinary and intestinal tract muscles of very young puppies are not fully developed. Therefore, like human babies, puppies need to relieve themselves frequently.

Take your puppy out often—every hour for an eight-week-old, for example. The older the puppy, the less often he'll need to relieve himself. Finally, as a mature, healthy adult, he'll require only three to five relief trips per day.

*The Nylabone® Foldaway Carrier is a useful tool for housetraining and traveling.*

*Your Poodle's outdoor needs will change as he matures. A healthy adult dog should require only three to five relief trips a day.*

## Housing

Because the type of housing and control you provide for your puppy has a direct relationship on the success of housetraining, we consider the various aspects of both before we begin training.

Bringing a new puppy home and turning him loose in your house can be compared to turning a child loose in a sports arena and telling the child the place is all his! The sheer enormity of the place would be too much for him to handle.

Instead, offer the puppy clearly defined areas where he can play, sleep, eat, and live. A room of the house where the family gathers the most is the obvious choice. Puppies are social animals and need to feel that they are a part of the pack right from the start. Hearing your voice, watching you while you're doing things, and smelling you nearby are all positive reinforcers that he is now a member of your pack. Usually a family room, the kitchen, or a nearby adjoining breakfast nook is ideal for providing safety and security for both puppy and owner.

Within that room, there should be a smaller area that the puppy can call his own. A cubby hole, a wire or fiberglass dog crate, or a fenced (not boarded) corner from which he can view the activities of his new family will be fine.

The size of the area or crate is the key factor here. The area must be large enough for the puppy to lay down and stretch out as well as stand up without rubbing his head on the top, yet small enough so that he cannot relieve himself at one end and sleep at the other without coming into contact with his droppings.

Dogs are, by nature, clean animals and will not remain close to their relief areas unless forced to do so. In those cases, they then become dirty dogs and usually remain that way for life.

By providing sleeping and resting quarters that fit the dog, and by offering frequent opportunities for him to relieve himself outside his quarters, the puppy quickly learns that the outdoors (or the newspaper if you're training him to paper) is the place to go when he needs to urinate or defecate. It also reinforces his innate desire to keep his sleeping quarters clean. This, in turn, helps develop the control muscles that will eventually produce a dog with clean living habits.

*A Nylabone® Flexible FRISBEE® disc will occupy your Poodle when he's out of his crate.*

The crate or cubby should be lined with a clean towel and no more than one toy should be placed in it. Do not put food or water in the crate, as eating and drinking will activate his digestive processes and ultimately defeat your purpose as well as make the puppy very uncomfortable as he attempts to "hold it."

Never line his sleeping area with newspaper. Puppy litters are usually raised on newspaper and, once in your home, the puppy will

*Dogs are clean animals by nature, and the Poodle is no exception.*

immediately associate newspaper with eliminating. Never put newspaper on any floor while housetraining as this will only confuse the puppy. If you're paper training him, use paper in his designated relief area only. Finally, restrict water intake after evening meals. Offer a few licks at a time—never let a young puppy gulp water after meals.

In addition to his crate, you may want to provide a soft bed for your puppy that he can use at will whenever he's in the house but not in his crate. A bean bag bed is ideal for this purpose. Oval wicker baskets are nice, but offer too much opportunity for destructive chewing. The soft wicker sides are usually right at the level of the dog's mouth.

When he's in his soft bed, perhaps chewing on a toy, you must supervise him and take the bed away if he decides to use it as a chew toy. Waiting until he's completed the teething process will assure that he doesn't develop bad habits of chewing on furniture. (And some Poodles seem to be real tenacious chewers!)

Save his soft bed for later months and years. (My own little Miniature, Ginger, was four years old before she could have a soft pillow in her crate because she was one of those serious chewers. Until then she was relegated to towels and she periodically shredded them into bits as well!)

Speaking of furniture, it's wise to decide before you bring your puppy home whether or not you intend to allow him on your furniture. Remember that if you allow him on the furniture as a puppy you'll have to do it when he's an adult.

Poodles don't shed hair onto furniture or clothes so most Poodle owners do allow their dogs on their furniture. However, if you have any reservations about this, set your rules now and stick to them. The puppy can and will adjust to your wishes providing you let him know what you do and don't want and remain consistent in your decision.

If you decide that the furniture should be reserved for people, then teach him from the beginning that sofas, chairs, and human beds are off limits. When he attempts to jump up onto a piece of furniture, say "No, off!" in a stern voice and remove him immediately. If he looks at you and turns away, tell him he's a "good boy!"

If he persists on jumping on a particular piece of furniture, gather a collection of hard objects, such as telephone books, canned goods, pots and pans, and literally cover the seat with the objects. Say nothing to the dog and set up this little trap while he's out of sight.

The next time the puppy goes to jump onto the furniture, he'll be faced with an array of clanging and uncomfortable items that prohibit him from making himself at home. Chances are, he'll jump off to the comfort and safety of the floor at which point you can tell him what a good boy he is.

Don't recognize his attempt to get on the furniture, but do recognize his being on the floor. Remember that recognizing positive behavior and ignoring negative behavior is a lot more successful in developing desirable habits.

## Control

By control we mean helping the puppy to create a lifestyle pattern that will be compatible to that of his human pack (you!). Just as we guide little children to learn our way of life, we must show the puppy when it's time to play, eat, sleep, exercise, and even entertain himself.

Your puppy should always sleep in his crate. He should also learn that during times of household confusion and excessive human

*Sheba loves joining Nicole and a friend in the pool.*

activity, such as breakfast time when family members are preparing for the day, he can play by himself in relative safety and comfort in his crate. Each time you leave the puppy alone, he should be crated. Puppies are chewers. They can't tell the difference between lamp cords, television wires, shoes, table legs, etc. If the puppy chews on the arm of a chair when he's alone, you will probably discipline him angrily when you get home. Thus, he makes the association that your coming home means he's going to be hit or punished. He won't remember chewing up the chair and is incapable of making the association of the discipline with his naughty deed. Give him plenty of Nylabones® to provide a positive chewing alternative.

Other times of excitement, such as family parties, etc., can be fun for the puppy providing he can view the activities from the security of his crate. He's not underfoot, he's not being fed all sorts of tidbits that will probably cause him stomach distress, yet he still feel like he's a part of the fun.

If you have a small child in the home who wants to get into the puppy's food bowl every time he eats, feeding the pup in his

*Make sure you puppy-proof your home so the naturally curious Poodle won't be able to get into trouble.*

crate is the answer. The child can't disturb the dog, and the pup will be free to eat in peace.

*The closer you stick to the schedule you set up for your puppy, the faster he'll be housetrained.*

## Schedule

As stated earlier, a puppy should be taken to his relief area each time he's released from his crate, after meals, after play sessions, when he first awakens in the morning (at 8 weeks of age this can mean 5 a.m.), and whenever he indicates by circling or sniffing busily that he needs to urinate or defecate. For puppies under ten weeks of age, a routine of taking him out every hour is necessary. As the puppy grows, he'll be able to wait for longer periods of time.

Keep trips to his relief area short. Stay no more than five or six minutes and then return to the house. If he goes during that time, praise him lavishly and take him indoors immediately. If he doesn't, but he has an accident when you go back indoors, pick him up immediately and say "No! No!" and return to his relief area. Wait a few minutes, then return to the house again. *Never* hit a puppy or rub his face in urine or excrement when he has an accident!

Once indoors, put the puppy in his crate until you've had time to clean up his accident. Then release him to the family area and watch him more closely than before. Chances are, his accident was a result of your not picking up his signal or waiting too long before offering him the opportunity to relieve himself. *Never* hold a grudge against the puppy for accidents.

Your puppy should also have regular play and exercise sessions when he's with you or a family member. Exercise for a very young puppy can consist of a short walk around the house or yard. Playing can include fetching games with a ball. Remember to restrict play periods to indoors within his living area (the family room for example) until he's completely housetrained.

Let the puppy learn that going outdoors means it's time to relieve himself, not play. Once trained, he'll be able to play indoors and out and still differentiate between the times for play and the times for relief.

Help him develop regular hours for naps, being alone, playing by himself, and just resting, all in his crate. Encourage him to entertain himself while you're busy with your activities. Let him learn that having you near is comforting, but your main purpose in life is not to provide him with undivided attention.

Each time you put the puppy in his crate, tell him, "It's cubby time!" (or whatever command you choose). Soon, he'll run to his crate when he hears you say those words.

In the beginning of his training, don't leave him in his crate for prolonged periods of time except during the night when everyone is sleeping. Make his experiences with his crate pleasant ones and, as an adult, he'll love it and willingly stay in it for several hours. (There are millions of people who go to work every day and leave their adult dogs crated while they're away. The dogs accept this as their lifestyle and look forward to "crate time.")

Crate training provides safety for you, the puppy, and the home. It also provides the puppy with a feeling of security, which helps a puppy develop self-confidence and clean habits.

## SIX STEPS TO SUCCESSFUL CRATE TRAINING

Remember, one of the primary ingredients in housetraining your puppy is control. Regardless of your lifestyle, there will always be occasions when you'll need to have a place where your dog can stay and be happy and safe. Crate training is the answer for now and in the future.

The following are step-by-step directions to actually training your puppy to accept his crate as his den, a place of security and comfort. Follow each step in order and don't try to rush the final steps. A conscientious approach to training will result in a happy dog that willingly accepts your lifestyle as his own.

1. Tell the puppy, "It's cubby time!" and place him in the crate with a small treat (a piece of cheese or half a biscuit). Let him lay in the crate for five minutes while you are in the same room. Then release him and praise lavishly. Never release him when he's fussing. Wait until he's quiet before you let him out.

2. Repeat step one several times a day.

3. The next day, place the puppy in the crate as before. Let him stay there for ten minutes. Do this several times.

4. Continue building time in 5-minute increments until the puppy will stay in his crate for 30 minutes with you in the room. Always take him to his relief area after prolonged periods in his crate.

5. Now go back to the beginning and let the puppy stay in his crate for five minutes while you are out of the room.

6. Once again, build crate time in five-minute increments with you out of the room. When the puppy will stay willingly in his crate (he may even fall asleep!) for 30 minutes with you out of the room he'll be ready to stay in it for several hours at a time.

In conclusion, a few key elements are really all you need for a successful house and crate training method: consistency, frequency, praise, control, and supervision. By following these procedures with a normal, healthy puppy, you and the puppy will soon be past the stage of "accidents" and ready to move on to a full and rewarding life together.

*Your Poodle will go through many different stages. Provide him with the proper care and guidance to ensure him a happy life.*

## CANINE DEVELOPMENT SCHEDULE

**First Through Third Period**—birth through seven weeks of age.

During this stage, a puppy needs food, sleep, and warmth and responds to simple and gentle touching. He needs his mother for security and discipline and his littermates for learning how to interact with other dogs. He also learns how to function within a pack and the pack order of dominance. Socializing the pup with adults and children for short periods will help him become aware of his environment.

**Fourth Period**—8 through 12 weeks.

A pup's brain is fully developed at this stage and he needs socializing with outside world. Remove him from his mother and littermates because he needs to change from canine pack to human pack. Human dominance is necessary. A fear period occurs between 8 and 16 weeks of age. Avoid fright and pain.

**Fifth Period**—13 through 16 weeks weeks of age.

Training and formal obedience should begin at this stage. Less association with other dogs and more with people, places, and

*A selection of Nylabone® chew toys should occupy your dog, but be careful to give him one favorite at a time once he's shown you what he likes best.*

situations should take place. This period will pass easily if you remember that this is a pup's change-to-adolescence time. Be firm and fair. The flight instinct is prominent. Per-missiveness and over-dis-ciplining can do permanent damage. Praise your pup for good behavior.

**Juvenile Period**—four months to eight months af age.

Another fear period about seven to eight months of age. It passes quickly, but be cautious of fright and pain. Sexual maturity is reached and dominant traits are established. The dog should understand sit, down, come, and stay at this stage.

Note: These are approximate time frames. Allow for individual differences in puppies.

*By the time your Poodle is seven or eight months of age, he should understand the sit, down, come, and stay commands.*

## Obedience Training

Finally, let's talk about training your Poodle. If you recall our earlier discussion and analysis of intelligence, you know that Poodles are the epitome of learning ability. As such, they should never be allowed to vegetate or become couch potatoes. The subsequent boredom that doing nothing produces can easily cause them to get into all kinds of mischief. Instead, put those bright minds and capable bodies to work—let them be useful members of your pack, teach them to entertain, and give them the opportunity to participate in sporting activities. Do something!

In my book *Training Your Dog for Sports and Other Activities* published by T.F.H. Publications, Inc., I offer over 30 activities from which to choose for your dog. Many of them are ideal things for Poodles to do.

You'll want to begin your Poodle puppy's training by enrolling him in a puppy class. Kindergarten classes are for puppies from 8 to 20 weeks of age and teach the puppy good manners, what is and

*Think of training as a way of teaching your Poodle how to communicate with you effectively.*

what is not acceptable behavior, and that you are the pack leader.

Beginner's obedience classes are for puppies five months and older. The lessons are similar and both classes, when taught by knowledgeable and caring instructors, help you and your puppy build a bond together that will last a lifetime.

Your puppy will learn to sit, stand, down, come, and stay on command. He'll learn to accept other dogs and people with gentleness and respect. He'll learn not to jump on people and to sit quietly for attention when your friends wish to greet him.

Poodles do not respond well to rough training methods. They are bright and need only to be shown a few times what you want them to do and they'll do it forever for your praise.

When searching for a good training facility, be sure the school has a reputation for enforc-ing humane and gentle training methods. Ask your veterinarian, friends, and other dog owners for references. Observe a class in session if you can and evaluate what you see. Are the dogs happy? Are the owners and dogs working well together? Are the teachers friendly and helpful?

*If you work slowly, surely and safely, you can teach your Poodle all sorts of things. This one perches on a ladder.*

When you've completed your Poodle's basic training, he'll be ready to discover some of the activities in my book. Try teaching your Poodle some tricks and how to be a home helper for starters. As you and your dog become experienced at learning together, you'll discover a wondrous world out there.

Remember the characters at the party? Whether your new Poodle is a chubby baby, a gangly adolescent, or a regal adult, you'll discover as you live with him that he's got a personality all his own. Whether he's a charmer or a clown, an acrobat or an actor, he will surprise and delight you every day of his life. So have fun at the party—he's a Poodle!

# SPORT of Purebred Dogs

Welcome to the exciting and sometimes frustrating sport of dogs. No doubt you are trying to learn more about dogs or you wouldn't be deep into this book. This section covers the basics that may entice you, further your knowledge, and help you to understand the dog world.

Dog showing has been a very popular sport for a long time and has been taken quite seriously by some. Others only enjoy it as a hobby.

The Kennel Club in England was formed in 1859, the American Kennel Club was established in 1884, and the Canadian Kennel Club was formed in 1888. The purpose of these clubs was to register purebred dogs and maintain their stud books. In the beginning, the concept of registering dogs was not readily accepted. More than 36 million dogs have been enrolled in the AKC Stud Book since its inception in 1888. Presently, the kennel clubs not only register dogs, but adopt and enforce rules and regulations governing dog shows, obedience trials, and field trials. Over the years they have fostered and encouraged interest in the health and welfare of the purebred dog. They routinely donate funds to veterinary research for study on genetic disorders.

Below are the addresses of the kennel clubs in the United States, Great Britain, and Canada.

American Kennel Club
260 Madison Avenue
New York, NY 10016
or 5580 Centerview Drive,
Raleigh, NC 27606

The Kennel Club
1 Clarges Street
Picadilly, London, WIY 8AB, England

The Canadian Kennel Club
89 Skyway Avenue
Suite 100
Etobicoke, Ontario, Canada M9W 6R4

Today there are numerous activities that are enjoyable for both the dog and the handler. Some of the activities include conformation showing, obedience competition, tracking, agility, the Canine Good Citizen® Certificate, and a wide range of instinct tests that vary from breed to breed. Where you start depends upon your goals, which early on may not be readily apparent.

## Puppy Kindergarten

Every puppy will benefit from this class. PKT is the foundation for all future dog activities from conformation to "couch potatoes." Pet owners should make an effort to attend, even if they never expect to show their dogs. The class is designed for puppies about three months of age with graduation at approximately five months of age. All the puppies will be in the same age group, and, even though some may be a little unruly, there should not be any real problem. This class will teach the puppy some beginning obedience. As in all obedience classes, the owner learns how to train his own dog. The PKT class gives the puppy the opportunity to interact with other puppies in the same age group and exposes him to strangers, which is very important. Some dogs grow up with behavior problems, one of them being fear of strangers. As you can see, there can be much to gain from this class.

There are some basic obedience exercises that every dog should learn. Some of these can be started with puppy kindergarten.

*A posse of Poodles poses for their owners at Camp Gone to the Dogs in Vermont.*

### Sit

One way of teaching the sit is to have your dog on your left side, with the leash in your right hand, close to the collar. Pull up on the leash, and at the same time reach around his hindlegs with your left hand and tuck them in. As you are doing this say, "Rover, sit." Always use the dog's name when you give an active command. Some owners like to use a treat, holding it over the dog's head. The dog will need to sit to get the treat. Encourage the dog to hold the sit for a few seconds, which will eventually be the beginning of the sit/stay. Depending on how cooperative he is, you can rub him under the chin or stroke his back. It is a good time to establish eye contact.

### Down

Sit the dog on your left side, and kneel down beside him with the leash in your right hand. Reach over him with your left hand and grasp his left foreleg. With your right hand, take his right foreleg and pull his legs forward while you say, "Rover, down." If he tries to get up, lean on his shoulder to encourage him to stay down. It will relax your dog if you stroke his back while he is down. Try to encourage him to stay down for a few seconds as preparation for the down/stay.

### Heel

The definition of heeling is the dog walking under control at your left heel. Your puppy will learn controlled walking in the puppy kindergarten class, which will eventually lead to heeling. Give the command "Rover, heel," and start off briskly with your left foot. Your leash is in your right hand, and your left hand is holding it about half way down. Your left hand should be able to control the leash, and there should be a little slack in it. You want him to walk with you with your leg somewhere between his nose and his shoulder. You need to encourage him to stay with you, not forging ahead or lagging behind you. It is best to keep him on a fairly short lead. Do not allow the lead to become tight. It is far better to give him a little jerk when necessary and remind him to heel. When you come to a halt, be prepared to physically make him sit. It takes practice to become coordinated. There are excellent books on training that you may wish to purchase. Your instructor should be able to recommend one for you.

*You'll need to study handling and grooming procedures if you want your Poodle to compete in the show ring.*

### Recall

Recall quite possibly is the most important exercise you will ever teach. It should be a pleasant experience. The puppy may learn to do random recalls while being attached to a long line such as a clothes line. Later, the exercise will start with the dog sitting and staying until called. The command is "Rover, come." Let your command be happy. You want your dog to come willingly and faithfully. The recall could save his life if he sneaks out the door. In practicing the recall, let him jump on you or touch you before you reach for him. If he is shy, then kneel down to his level. Reaching for the insecure dog could frighten him, and he may not be willing to come again in the future. Lots of praise and a treat would be in order whenever you do a recall. Under no circumstances should you ever correct your dog when he has come to you. Later, in formal obedience, your dog will be required to sit in front of you after recalling and then go to heel position.

## CONFORMATION

Conformation showing is the oldest dog show sport. This type of showing is based on the dog's appearance—that is his structure, movement, and attitude. When considering this type of showing, you need to be aware of your breed's standard and be able to evaluate your dog compared to that standard. The breeder of your puppy or other experienced breeders would be good sources for such an evaluation. Puppies can go through lots of changes over a period of time. Many puppies start out as promising hopefuls and then after maturing may be disappointing as show candidates. Even so, this should not deter them from being excellent pets.

Conformation training classes are usually offered by the local kennel or obedience clubs. These are excellent places for training puppies. The puppy should be able to walk on a lead before entering such a class. Proper ring procedure and technique for posing (stacking) the dog will be demonstrated, as well as gaiting the dog. Generally, certain patterns are used in the ring, such as the triangle or the "L." Conformation class, like the PKT class, will give your youngster the opportunity to socialize with different breeds of dog and humans, too.

It takes some time to learn the routine of conformation showing. Usually, one starts at the puppy matches that may be AKC sanctioned or fun matches. These matches are generally for puppies

*Dogs compete against dogs and bitches against bitches in the regular classes. Both are pared down until there's just one Best of Breed winner.*

from 2 or 3 months to a year old, and there may be classes for the adult over the age of 12 months. Similar to point shows, the classes are divided by sex, and after completion of the classes in that breed or variety, the class winners compete for Best of Breed or Variety. The winner goes on to compete in the Group, and the Group winners compete for Best in Match. No championship points are awarded for match wins.

A few matches can be great training for puppies, even if there is no intention to go on showing. Matches enable the puppy to meet new people and be handled by a stranger—the judge. It also offers a change of environment, which broadens the horizon for both dog and handler. Matches and other dog activities boost the confidence of the handler, and especially the younger handlers.

Earning an AKC championship is built on a point system, which is different from Great Britain. To become an AKC Champion of Record, the dog must earn 15 points. The number of points earned each time depends upon the number of dogs in competition. The number of points available at each show depends upon the breed, its sex, and the location of the show. The United States is divided into ten AKC zones. Each zone has its own set of points. The purpose of the zones is to try to equalize the points available from breed to breed and area to area.The AKC adjusts the point scale annually.

The number of points that can be won at a show are between one and five. Three-, four-, and five-point wins are considered majors. Not only does the dog need 15 points won under 3 different judges, but those points must include 2 majors under 2 different judges. Canada also works on a point system, but majors are not required.

Males always show before bitches. The classes available to those seeking points are: Puppy (which may be divided into 6 to 9 months and 9 to 12 months); 12 to 18 months; Novice; Bred-by-Exhibitor; American-bred; and Open. The class winners of the same sex of each breed or variety compete against each other for Winners Dog and Winners Bitch. A Reserve Winners Dog and Reserve Winners Bitch are also awarded but do not carry any points unless the Winners win is disallowed by AKC. The Winners Dog and Bitch compete with the Specials (those dogs that have attained championship) for Best of Breed or Variety, Best of Winners, and Best of Opposite Sex. It is possible to pick up an extra point or even a major if the points are higher for the defeated winner than those of Best of Winners. The latter would get the higher total from the defeated winner.

At an all-breed show, each Best of Breed or Variety winner will go on to his respective Group and then the Group winners will compete against each other for Best in Show. There are seven Groups: Sporting, Hounds, Working, Terriers, Toys, Non-Sporting, and Herding. Obviously, there are no Groups at speciality shows (those shows that have only one breed or a show such as the American Spaniel Club's Flushing Spaniel Show, which is for all flushing spaniel breeds).

*Outdoor shows are the best places for seeing the dogs and meeting their owners.*

Earning a championship in England is somewhat different since they do not have a point system. Challenge Certificates are awarded if the judge feels the dog is deserving, regardless of the number of dogs in competition. A dog must earn 3 Challenge Certificates under 3 different judges, with at least 1 of these Certificates being won after the age of 12 months. Competition is very strong and entries may be higher than they are in the US. The Kennel Club's Challenge Certificates are only available at championship shows.

*As a handler, you shouldn't detract from your dog's appearance. Wear neat but practical attire.*

In England, The Kennel Club regulations require that certain dogs, Border Collies and gundog breeds, qualify in a working capacity (i.e., obedience or field trials) before becoming a full champion. If they do not qualify in the working aspect, then they are designated a show champion, which is equivalent to the AKC's Champion of Record. A gundog may be granted the title of Field Trial Champion (FTCh.) if he passes all the tests in the field, but would also have to qualify in conformation before becoming a full champion. A Border Collie that earns the title of Obedience Champion (ObCh.) must also qualify in the conformation ring before becoming a champion.

The US doesn't have a designation full Champion, but does award for Dual and Triple Champions. The Dual Champion must be a Champion of Record, and either Champion Tracker, Herding Champion, Obedience Trial Champion, or Field Champion. Any dog that has been awarded the titles of Champion of Record, and any two of the following: Champion Tracker, Herding Champion, Obedience Trial Champion or Field Champion, may be designated as a Triple Champion.

The shows in England seem to put more emphasis on breeder judges than those in the US. There is much competition within the breeds. Therefore, the quality of the individual breeds should be very good. In the US we tend to have more "all around judges," (those that judge multiple breeds) and use the breeder judges at the specialty shows. Breeder judges are more familiar with their own breed as they are actively breeding that breed or did so at one time. Americans emphasize Group and Best in Show wins and promote them accordingly.

The shows in England can be very large and extend over several days, with the Groups being scheduled on different days. Though multi-day shows are not common in the US, there are cluster shows in which several different clubs will use the same show site over consecutive days.

Westminster Kennel Club is our most prestigious show, although the entry is limited to 2500. In recent years, entry has been limited to champions. This show is more formal than the majority of the shows, with the judges wearing formal attire and the handlers fashionably dressed. In most instances, the quality of the dogs is superb. After all, it is a show of champions. It is a good show to study the AKC registered breeds and is by far the most exciting—especially since it is televised! WKC is one of the few shows in this country that is still benched. This means the dog must be in his benched area during the show hours, except when he is being groomed, is in the ring, or is being exercised.

Typically, the handlers are very particular about their appearances. They are careful not to wear something that will detract from their dogs, but will perhaps enhance them. American ring procedure is quite formal compared to that of other countries. There is a certain etiquette expected between the judge and exhibitor and among the other exhibitors. Of course, it is not always the case, but the judge is supposed to be polite, not engaging in small talk or acknowledging how well he knows the handler. There is a more informal and relaxed atmosphere at the shows in other countries. For instance, the dress code is more casual. I can see where this might be more fun for the exhibitor and especially for the novice. The US is very handler-oriented in many of the breeds. It is true, in most instances, that the experienced professional handler can better present the dog and will have a feel for what a judge likes.

In England, Crufts is The Kennel Club's own show and is most assuredly the largest dog show in the world. It's been known to have an entry of nearly 20,000, and the show lasts four days. Entry is only gained by qualifying through winning in specified classes at another championship show. Westminster is strictly conformation, but Crufts exhibitors and spectators enjoy not only conformation, but obedience, agility, and a multitude of exhibitions, as well. Obedience was admitted in 1957 and agility in 1983.

If you are handling your own dog, please give some consideration to your apparel. The dress code at matches is more informal than at the point shows. However, you should wear something a little more appropriate than beach attire or ragged jeans and bare feet. If you check out the handlers and see what is presently fashionable, you'll catch on. Men usually dress with a shirt and tie and a nice sports coat. Whether you are male or female, you will want to wear comfortable clothes and shoes. You need to be able to run with your dog, and you certainly don't want to take a chance of falling and hurting yourself. Heaven forbid, if nothing else, you'll upset your dog. Women usually wear a dress or two-piece outfit, preferably with pockets to carry bait, brush, etc. In this case, men are the lucky ones with all their pockets. Ladies, think about where your dress will be if you need to kneel on the floor, and also think about running. Does it allow freedom to do so?

You need to take along dog; crate; ex pen (if you use one); extra bedding; water pail and water; all required grooming equipment; table; chair for you; bait for dog and lunch for you and friends; and,

*A Canine Good Citizen® needs to know how to sit politely for petting.*

last but not least, clean up materials, such as plastic bags, paper towels, and perhaps a damp towel—just in case. Don't forget your entry confirmation and directions to the show.

If you are showing in obedience, you may want to wear pants. Many of our top obedience handlers wear pants that are color-coordinated with their dogs. The philosophy is that imperfections in the black dog will be less obvious next to your black pants.

Whether you are showing in conformation, Junior Showmanship, or obedience, you need to watch the clock and be sure you are not late. It is customary to pick up your conformation armband a few minutes before the start of the class. They will not wait for you, and if you are on the show grounds and not in the ring, you will upset everyone. It's a little more complicated picking up your obedience armband if you show later in the class. If you have not picked it up and they get to your number, you may not be allowed to show. It's best to pick up your armband early, but be aware that you may show earlier than expected if other handlers don't pick up. Customarily, all conflicts should be discussed with the judge prior to the start of the class.

*A long sit is part of the basic obedience exercises required to earn a Companion Dog (CD) title from the AKC.*

*This Poodle shows perfect form over the high jump, used in exercises for advanced obedience titles.*

## Canine Good Citizen®

The AKC sponsors a program to encourage dog owners to train their dogs. Local clubs perform the pass/fail tests, and dogs that pass are awarded a Canine Good Citizen® Certificate. Proof of vaccination is required at the time of participation. The test includes:

1. Accepting a friendly stranger.
2. Sitting politely for petting.
3. Appearance and grooming.
4. Walking on a loose leash.
5. Walking through a crowd.
6. Sit and down on command/staying in place.
7. Come when called.
8. Reaction to another dog.
9. Reactions to distractions.
10. Supervised separation.

If more effort was made by pet owners to accomplish these exercises, fewer dogs would be cast off to the humane shelter.

*The tire jump on an agility course is no obstacle for this white Miniature.*

## OBEDIENCE

Obedience is necessary, without a doubt, but it can also become a wonderful hobby or even an obsession. Obedience classes and competition can provide wonderful companionship, not only with your dog but with your classmates or fellow competitors. It is always gratifying to discuss your dog's problems with others who have had similar experiences. The AKC acknowledged obedience around 1936, and it has changed tremendously even though many of the exercises are basically the same. Today, obedience competition is just that—very competitive. Even so, it is possible for every obedience exhibitor to come home a winner (by earning qualifying scores), even though he/she may not earn a placement in the class.

Most of the obedience titles are awarded after earning three qualifying scores (legs) in the appropriate class under three different judges. These classes offer a perfect score of 200, which is extremely rare. Each of the class exercises has its own point value. A leg is earned after receiving a score of at least 170 and at least 50 percent of the points available in each exercise. The titles are:

**Companion Dog—CD**

This is called the Novice Class and the exercises are:

| | |
|---|---|
| 1. Heel on leash and figure 8 | 40 points |
| 2. Stand for examination | 30 points |
| 3. Heel free | 40 points |
| 4. Recall | 30 points |
| 5. Long sit—one minute | 30 points |
| 6. Long down—three minutes | 30 points |
| Maximum total score | 200 points |

**Companion Dog Excellent—CDX**

This is the Open Class and the exercises are:

| | |
|---|---|
| 1. Heel off leash and figure 8 | 40 points |
| 2. Drop on recall | 30 points |
| 3. Retrieve on flat | 20 points |
| 4. Retrieve over high jump | 30 points |
| 5. Broad jump | 20 points |
| 6. Long sit—three minutes (out of sight) | 30 points |
| 7. Long down—five minutes (out of sight) | 30 points |
| Maximum total score | 200 points |

**Utility Dog—UD**

The Utility Class exercises are:

| | |
|---|---|
| 1. Signal exercise | 40 points |
| 2. Scent discrimination-Article 1 | 30 points |
| 3. Scent discrimination-Article 2 | 30 points |
| 4. Directed retrieve | 30 points |
| 5. Moving stand and examination | 30 points |
| 6. Directed jumping | 40 points |
| Maximum total score | 200 points |

After achieving the UD title, you may feel inclined to go after the UDX and/or OTCh. The UDX (Utility Dog Excellent) title went into effect in January 1994. It is not easily attained. The title requires qualifying simultaneously ten times in Open B and Utility B, but not necessarily at consecutive shows.

The OTCh. (Obedience Trial Champion) is awarded after the dog has earned his UD and then goes on to earn 100 championship points, a first place in Utility, a first place in Open, and another first place in either class. The placements must be won under three different judges at all-breed obedience trials. The points are determined by the number of dogs competing in the Open B and Utility B classes. The OTCh. title precedes the dog's name.

Obedience matches (AKC-sanctioned, fun, and show and go) are often available. Usually, they are sponsored by the local obedience clubs. When preparing an obedience dog for a title, you will find matches very helpful. Fun matches and show and go matches are more lenient in allowing you to make corrections in the ring. This type of training is usually very necessary for the Open and Utility classes. AKC-sanctioned obedience matches do not allow corrections in the ring since they must abide by the AKC obedience regulations booklet. If you are interested in showing in obedience, you should contact the AKC for a copy of *Obedience Regulations.*

## AGILITY

Agility was first introduced by John Varley at the Crufts Dog Show in England in February 1978, but Peter Meanwell, competitor and judge, actually developed the idea. It was officially recognized in the early '80s. Agility is extremely popular in England and

*Rudy tackles the agility course Dog Walk—similar to the balance beam in gymnastics.*

*This chocolate Poodle shows an abundance of talent for the bar jump on an agility course.*

Canada and growing in popularity in the US. The AKC acknowledged agility in August 1994. Dogs must be at least 12 months of age to be entered. It is a fascinating sport that the dog, handler, and spectators enjoy to the utmost. Agility is a spectator sport! The dog performs off lead. The handler either runs with his dog or positions himself on the course. He then directs his dog with verbal and hand signals over a timed course, over or through a variety of obstacles, including a time out or pause. One of the main drawbacks to agility is finding a place to train. The obstacles take up a lot of space, and it is very time consuming to put up and take down courses.

The titles earned at AKC agility trials are Novice Agility Dog (NAD), Open Agility Dog (OAD), Agility Dog Excellent (ADX), and Master Agility Excellent (MAX). In order to acquire an agility title, a dog must earn a qualifying score in his respective class on three separate occasions under two different judges. The MAX will be awarded after earning ten qualifying scores in the Agility Excellent Class.

*Rewarding your Poodle with a fun Nylabone® is a good way to end a training session.*

### General Information

Obedience, tracking, and agility allow the purebred dog with an Indefinite Listing Privilege (ILP) number or a limited registration to be exhibited and earn titles. Application must be made to the AKC for an ILP number.

The American Kennel Club publishes *Events*, a monthly magazine that is part of the *Gazette*, their official journal for the sport of purebred dogs. The *Events* section lists upcoming shows and the secretary or superintendent for them. The majority of the conformation shows in the US are overseen by licensed superintendents. Generally, the entry closing date is approximately two-and-a-half weeks before the actual show. Point shows are fairly expensive, while the match shows cost about one-third of the point show entry fee. Match shows usually take entries the day of the show, but some are pre-entry. The best way to find match show information is through your local kennel club. Upon asking, the AKC can provide you with a list of superintendents, and you can write and ask to be put on their mailing lists.

Obedience trial and tracking test information is also available through the AKC. Frequently, these events are not superintended, but put on by the host club. Therefore, you would make the entry with the event's secretary.

There are numerous activities you can share with your dog. Regardless of what you do, it does take teamwork. Your dog can only benefit from your attention and training. We hope this chapter has enlightened you and hope, if nothing else, you will attend a show here and there. Perhaps you will start with a puppy kindergarten class, and who knows where it may lead!

# HEALTH CARE

Veterinary medicine has become far more sophisticated than what was available to our ancestors. This can be attributed to the increase in household pets and, consequently, the demand for better care for them. Also, human medicine has become far more complex. Today, diagnostic testing in veterinary medicine parallels human diagnostics. Because of better technology, we can expect our pets to live healthier lives, thereby increasing their life spans.

## THE FIRST CHECKUP

You will want to take your new puppy/dog in for his first checkup within 48 to 72 hours after acquiring him. Many breeders strongly recommend this checkup and so do the humane shelters. A puppy/dog can appear healthy, but he may have a serious problem that is not apparent to the layman. Most pets have some type of a minor flaw that may never cause a real problem.

*This Poodle's full coat, clear eyes, white teeth, and alert expression are all signs of excellent health.*

Unfortunately, if he/she should have a serious problem, you will want to consider the consequences of keeping the pet and the attachments that will be formed, which may be broken prematurely. Keep in mind there are many healthy dogs looking for good homes.

This first checkup is a good time to establish yourself with the veterinarian and to learn the office policy regarding their hours and how they handle emergencies. Usually, the breeder or another conscientious pet owner is a good

*The Swiss Alps provide a stunning backdrop for these three Poodles resting on their hike.*

reference for locating a capable veterinarian. You should be aware that not all vets give the same quality of service. Please do not make your selection based on the least expensive clinic, as they may be shortchanging your pet. There is the possibility that it will eventually cost you more due to improper diagnosis, treatment, etc. If you are selecting a new veterinarian, feel free to ask for a tour of the clinic. You should inquire about making an appointment for a tour, because all clinics are working clinics, and therefore, may not be available all day for sightseers. You may worry less if you see where your pet will be spending the day if he ever needs to be hospitalized.

## The Physical Exam

Your veterinarian will check your pet's overall condition, which includes listening to the heart; checking the respiration; feeling the abdomen, muscles, and joints; checking the mouth, which includes gum color and signs of gum disease, along with plaque buildup; checking the ears for signs of an infection or ear mites; examining the eyes; and, last but not least, checking the condition of the skin and coat.

He should ask you questions regarding your pet's eating and elimination habits and invite you to relay your questions. It is a good idea to prepare a list so as not to forget anything. He should discuss the proper diet and the quantity to be fed. If this differs from your breeder's recommendation, you should convey to him what the breeder's choice is and see if he approves. If he recommends changing the diet, this should be done over a few days so as not to cause a gastrointestinal upset. It is customary to take in a fresh stool sample (just a small amount) to test for intestinal parasites. It must be fresh, preferably within 12 hours, because the eggs hatch quickly and after hatching will not be observed under the microscope. If your pet isn't obliging, the technician can usually take a sample in the clinic.

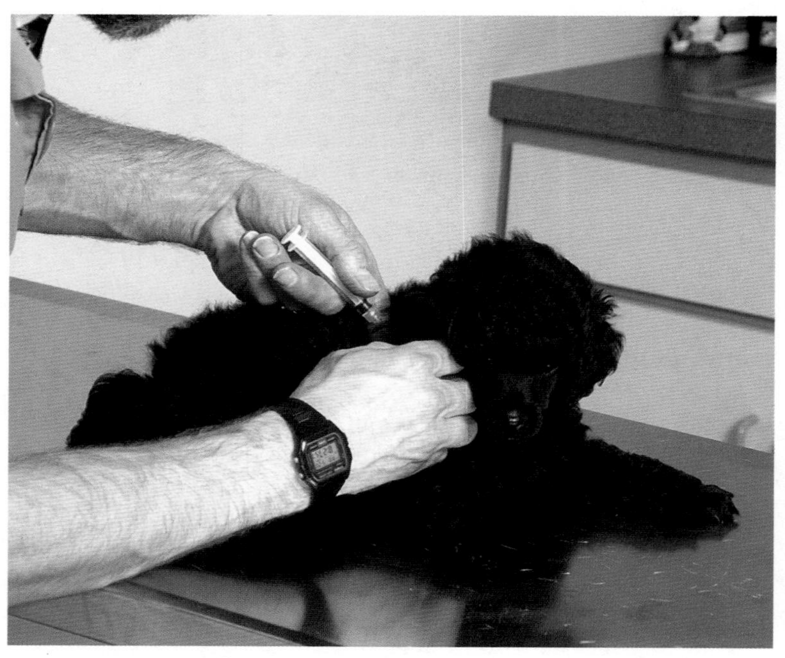

*Maintaining your Poodle's immunization schedule and booster shots will help him live a long and healthy life.*

*These two-week-old pups are still protected from some diseases by the antibodies in their mother's milk, but in a few more weeks they'll start getting shots from the vet.*

## Immunizations

It is important that you take your puppy/dog's vaccination record with you on your first visit. In the case of a puppy, presumably the breeder has seen to the vaccinations up to the time you acquired custody. Veterinarians differ in their vaccination protocol. It is not unusual for your puppy to have received vaccinations for distemper, hepatitis, leptospirosis, parvovirus, and parainfluenza every two to three weeks from the age of five or six weeks. Usually, this is a combined injection and is typically called the DHLPP. The DHLPP is given through at least 12 to 14 weeks of age, and it is customary to continue with another parvovirus vaccine at 16 to 18 weeks. You may wonder why so many immunizations are necessary. No one knows for sure when the puppy's maternal antibodies are gone, although it is customarily accepted that distemper antibodies are gone by 12 weeks. Usually, parvovirus antibodies are gone by 16 to 18 weeks of age. However, it is possible for the maternal antibodies to be gone much earlier or even at a later age. Therefore, immunizations are started at an early age. The vaccine will not give immunity as long as there are maternal antibodies.

The rabies vaccination is given at three or six months of age, depending on your local laws. A vaccine for bordetella (kennel cough) is advisable and can be given any time from the age of five weeks. The coronavirus is not commonly given unless there is a problem locally. The Lyme vaccine is necessary in endemic areas. Lyme disease has been reported in 47 states.

### Distemper

Distemper is virtually an incurable disease. If the dog recovers, he is subject to severe nervous disorders. The virus attacks every tissue in the body and resembles a bad cold with a fever. It can cause a runny nose and eyes and cause gastrointestinal disorders, including a poor appetite, vomiting, and diarrhea. The virus is carried by raccoons, foxes, wolves, mink, and other dogs. Unvaccinated youngsters and senior citizens are very susceptible. This is still a common disease.

### Hepatitis

Hepatitis is a virus that is most serious in very young dogs. It is spread by contact with an infected animal or its stool or urine. The virus affects the liver and kidneys and is characterized by high fever, depression, and lack of appetite. Recovered animals may be afflicted with chronic illnesses.

### Leptospirosis

Leptospirosis is a bacterial disease transmitted by contact with the urine of an infected dog, rat, or other wildlife. It produces severe symptoms of fever, depression, jaundice, and internal bleeding and was fatal before the vaccine was developed. Recovered dogs can be carriers, and the disease can be transmitted from dogs to humans.

### Parvovirus

Parvovirus was first noted in the late 1970s and is still a fatal disease. However, with proper vaccinations, early diagnosis, and prompt treatment, it is a manageable disease. It attacks the bone marrow and intestinal tract. The symptoms include depression, loss of appetite, vomiting, diarrhea, and collapse. Immediate medical attention is of the essence.

### Rabies

Rabies is shed in the saliva and is carried by raccoons, skunks, foxes, other dogs, and cats. It attacks nerve tissue, resulting in paralysis and death. Rabies can be transmitted to people and is virtually always fatal. This disease is reappearing in the suburbs.

### Bordetella (Kennel Cough)

The symptoms of bordetella are coughing, sneezing, hacking, and retching accompanied by nasal discharge usually lasting from a few days to several weeks. There are several disease-producing organisms responsible for this disease. The present vaccines are helpful but do not protect for all the strains. It usually is not life

*Dogs that share living quarters, including food or water dishes, are more susceptible to contagious diseases. Be sure to keep all bowls and water dishes clean.*

threatening, but in some instances it can progress to a serious bronchopneumonia. The disease is highly contagious. The vaccination should be given routinely for dogs that come into contact with other dogs, such as through boarding, training class, or visits to the groomer.

### Coronavirus

Coronavirus is usually self-limiting and not a life-threatening disease. It was first noted in the late '70s about a year before parvovirus. The virus produces a yellow/brown stool, and there may be depression, vomiting, and diarrhea.

### Lyme Disease

Lyme disease was first diagnosed in the United States in 1976 in Lyme, CT, in people who lived in close proximity to the deer tick. Symptoms may include acute lameness, fever, swelling of joints, and loss of appetite. Your veterinarian can advise you if you live in an endemic area.

*Dogs that spend time outdoors are susceptible to ticks. Check your Poodle's coat after he has been playing outside.*

### Booster Shots

After your puppy has completed his puppy vaccinations, you will continue to booster the DHLPP once a year. It is customary to booster the rabies one year after the first vaccine and then, depending on where you live, it should be boostered every year or every three years. This depends on your local laws. The Lyme and corona vaccines are boostered annually, and it is recommended that the bordetella be boostered every six to eight months.

*As your Poodle ages, his health needs will change. Keep veterinary visits regular and all vaccines up to date.*

## Annual Visit

I would like to stress the importance of the annual checkup, which would include booster vaccinations, a check for intestinal parasites, and a test for heartworm. Today, in our very busy world, it is rush, rush, and see "how much you can get for how little." Unbelievably, some nonveterinary establish-ments have entered into the vaccination business. More harm than good can come to your dog through improper vaccinations, possibly from inferior vaccines and/or the wrong schedule. More than likely, you truly care about your companion dog, and over the years you have devoted much time and expense to his well being. Perhaps you are unaware that a vaccination is not just a vaccination. There is more involved. Please follow through with regular physical examinations. It is so important for your veterinarian to know your dog, and this is especially true during middle age and through the geriatric years. Your older dog may require more than one physical a year. The annual physical is good preventive medicine. Through early diagnosis and subsequent treatment, your dog can maintain a longer and better quality of life.

*To ensure good health, this adorable puppy will be tested for internal parasites upon his first visit to the veterinarian.*

## Intestinal Parasites

*Keeping your Poodle safely contained while outside will prevent him from coming into contact with anything dangerous.*

### Hookworms

Hookworms are almost microscopic intestinal worms that can cause anemia and, therefore, serious problems, including death, in young puppies. Hookworms can be transmitted to humans through penetration of the skin. Puppies may be born with them.

### Roundworms

Roundworms are spaghetti-like worms that can cause a potbellied appearance and dull coat, along with more severe symptoms such as vomiting, diarrhea, and coughing. Puppies acquire these while in the mother's uterus and through lactation. Both hookworms and roundworms may be acquired through ingestion.

### Whipworms

Whipworms have a three-month life cycle and are not acquired through the dam. They cause intermittent diarrhea, usually with mucus. Whipworms are possibly the most difficult worm to eradicate. Their eggs are very resistant to most environmental factors and can last for years until the proper conditions enable them to mature. Whipworms are seldom seen in the stool.

Intestinal parasites are more prevalent in some areas than others. Climate, soil, and contamination are big factors contributing to the incidence of intestinal parasites. Eggs are passed in the stool, lay on the ground, and then become infective in a certain number of days. Each of the above worms has a different life cycle. Your dog's best chance of becoming and remaining worm-free is to always pooper-scoop your yard. A fenced-in yard keeps stray dogs out, which is certainly helpful.

Having a fecal examination done on your dog twice a year, or more often if there is a problem, is recommended. If your dog has a positive fecal sample, he will be given the appropriate medication and you will be asked to bring back another stool sample in a certain period of time (depending on the type of worm), and then he will be rewormed. This process goes on until he has at least two negative samples. Different types of worm require different medications. You will be wasting your money and doing your dog an injustice by buying over-the-counter medication without first consulting your veterinarian.

## OTHER INTERNAL PARASITES

### Coccidiosis and Giardiasis

Coccidiosis and giardiasis, which are protozoal infections, usually affect pups, especially in places where large numbers of puppies are brought together. Older dogs may harbor these infections, but do not show signs unless they are stressed. Symptoms include diarrhea, weight loss, and lack of appetite. These infections are not always apparent in the fecal examination.

### Tapeworms

Seldom apparent on fecal floatation, tapeworms are diagnosed frequently as rice-like segments around the dog's anus and the base of the tail. Tapeworms are long, flat, and ribbon-like, sometimes several feet in length, and made up of many segments about five-eighths of an inch long. The two most common causes of tapeworm found in the dog are:

(1) The larval form of the flea tapeworm parasite matures in an intermediate host, the flea, before it can become infective. Your dog acquires this by ingesting the flea through licking and chewing.

(2) Rabbits, rodents, and certain large game animals serve as intermediate hosts for other species of tapeworm. If your dog eats one of these infected hosts, he can acquire tapeworms.

## HEARTWORM DISEASE

Heartworm is a worm that resides in the heart and adjacent blood vessels of the lung that produces microfilaria, which circulate in the bloodstream. It is possible for a dog to be infected with any number of worms from 1 to a 100 that can be 6 to 14 inches long. It is a life-threatening disease, expensive to treat, and easily prevented. Depending on where you live, your veterinarian may recommend a preventive year-round and either an annual or semiannual blood test. The most common preventive is given once a month.

## External Parasites

### Fleas

Fleas are not only the dog's worst enemy, but also enemy to the owner's pocketbook. Preventing is less expensive than treating, but regardless, we'd prefer to spend our money elsewhere. Likely, the majority of our dogs are allergic to the bite of a flea, and in many cases, it only takes one flea bite. The protein in the flea's saliva is the culprit. Allergic dogs have a reaction, which usually results in a "hot spot." More than likely, such a reaction will involve a trip to the veterinarian for treatment. Yes, prevention is less expensive. Fortunately, today there are several good products available.

If there is a flea infestation, no one product is going to correct the problem. Not only will the dog require treatment, so will the environment. In general, flea collars are not very effective, although there is an "egg" collar now available that will kill the eggs on the dog. Dips are the most economical, but they are messy. There are

*A flea problem can easily get out of hand when fleas infest the dog and its environment. Be diligent about checking your Poodle for fleas.*

some effective shampoos and treatments available through pet shops and veterinarians. An oral tablet arrived on the American market in 1995 and was popular in Europe the previous year. It sterilizes the female flea, but will not kill adult fleas. Therefore, the tablet, which is given monthly, will decrease the flea population but is not a "cure-all." Those dogs that suffer from flea-bite allergy will still be subjected to the bite of the flea. Another popular parasiticide is permethrin, which is applied to the back of the dog in one or two places, depending on the dog's weight. This product works as a repellent, causing the flea to get "hot feet" and jump off. Do not confuse this product with some of the organophosphates that are also applied to the dog's back.

Some products are not usable on young puppies. Treating fleas should be done under your veterinarian's guidance. Frequently, it is necessary to combine products, and the layman does not have knowledge regarding possible toxicities. It is hard to believe, but there are a few dogs that do have a natural resistance to fleas. Nevertheless, it would be wise to treat all pets at the same time. Don't forget your cats. Cats just love to prowl the neighborhood, and, consequently, return with unwanted guests.

Adult fleas live on the dog, but their eggs drop off into the environment. There, they go through four larval stages before reaching adulthood, and thereby are able to jump back on the poor unsuspecting

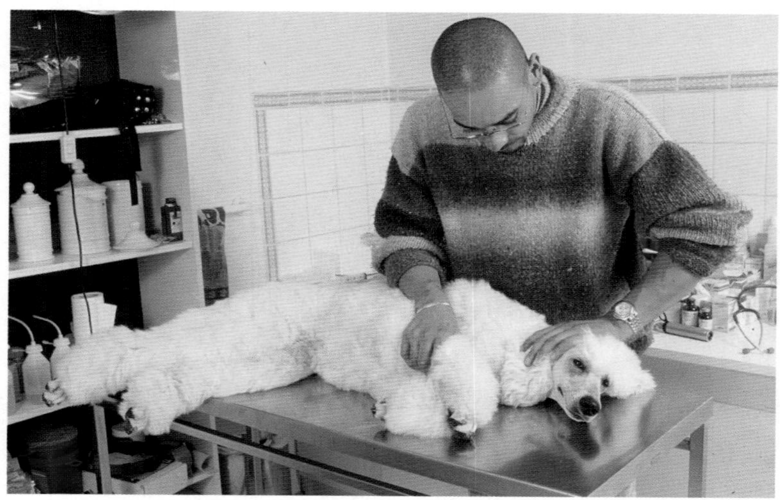

*Your Poodle will need regular veterinary visits to maintain his good health.*

dog. The cycle resumes and takes between 21 to 28 days under ideal conditions. There are environmental products available that will kill both adult fleas and larvae.

*Most breeders will ask that you have your pet spayed or neutered. Breeding requires a great deal of knowledge about the breed and should not be taken lightly.*

### Ticks

Ticks can carry Rocky Mountain Spotted Fever, Lyme disease, and can cause tick paralysis. They should be removed with tweezers. Try to pull out the head because the jaws carry disease. There is a tick preventive collar that does an excellent job. Ticks automatically back out on those dogs wearing collars.

### Sarcoptic Mange

Sarcoptic mange is a mite that is difficult to find on skin scrapings. The pinnal reflex is a good indicator of this disease. Rub the ends of the pinna (ear) together and the dog will start scratching with his foot. Sarcoptes are highly contagious to other dogs and to humans, although they do not live long on humans. They cause intense itching.

### Demodectic Mange

Demodectic mange is a mite that is passed from the dam to her puppies. It commonly affects youngsters aged three to ten months. Diagnosis is confirmed by skin scraping. Small areas of alopecia around the eyes, lips, and/or forelegs become visible. There is little itching, unless there is a secondary bacterial infection. Some breeds are afflicted more than others.

### Cheyletiella

Cheyletiella causes intense itching and is diagnosed by skin scraping. It lives in the outer layers of the skin of dogs, cats, rabbits, and humans. Yellow-gray scales may be found on the back and the rump, top of the head, and the nose.

## TO BREED OR NOT TO BREED

More than likely, your breeder has requested that you have your puppy neutered or spayed. Your breeder's request is based on what is healthiest for your dog and what is most beneficial for your breed. Experienced and conscientious breeders devote many years to developing a bloodline. In order to do this, they make every effort to plan each breeding in regard to conformation, temperament, and health. This type of breeder does his best to perform the necessary testing (i.e., OFA, CERF, testing for inherited blood disorders, thyroid, etc.). Testing is expensive and sometimes very disheartening when a favorite dog doesn't pass his health tests. The health history pertains not only to the breeding stock, but to the immediate ancestors. Reputable breeders do not want their offspring to be bred indiscriminately. Therefore, you may be asked to neuter or spay your puppy. Of course, there is always the exception, and the breeder may agree to let you breed your dog under his direct supervision. This is an important concept. More and more effort is being made to breed healthier dogs.

*Spaying or neutering your dog can decrease his or her chances of developing cancer of the reproductive organs.*

### Spay/Neuter

There are numerous benefits to spaying or neutering your dog at six months of age. Unspayed females are subject to mammary and ovarian cancer. In order to prevent mammary cancer, she must be spayed prior to her first heat cycle. Later in life, an unspayed female may develop a pyometra (an infected uterus), which is definitely life threatening.

*Neutered or spayed dogs can compete in all dog sports except conformation shows.*

Spaying is performed under a general an-esthetic and is easy on the young dog. As you might expect, it is a little harder on the older dog, but that is no reason to deny her the surgery. The surgery removes the ovaries and uterus. It is important to remove all the ovarian tissue. If some is left behind, she could remain attractive to males. In order to view the ovaries, a reasonably long incision is necessary. An ovario-hysterectomy is consid-ered major surgery.

Neutering the male at a young age will inhibit some characteristic male behavior that owners frown upon. Some boys will not hike their legs and mark territory if they are neutered at six months of age. Also, neutering at a young age has hormonal benefits, lessening the chance of hormonal aggressiveness.

Surgery involves removing the testicles but leaving the scrotum. If there should be a retained testicle, the male definitely needs to be neutered before the age of two or three years. Retained testicles can develop cancer. Unneutered males are at risk for testicular cancer, perineal fistulas, perianal tumors and fistulas, and prostatic disease.

Intact males and females may be prone to housetraining accidents. Females urinate frequently before, during, and after heat cycles, and males tend to mark territory if there is a female in heat. Males may show the same behavior if there is a visiting dog or guests.

Surgery involves a sterile operating procedure equivalent to human surgery. The incision site is shaved, surgically scrubbed, and draped. The veterinarian wears a sterile surgical gown, cap, mask, and gloves. Anesthesia should be monitored by a registered technician. It is customary for the veterinarian to recommend a pre-anesthetic blood screening, looking for metabolic problems, and an ECG rhythm strip to check for normal heart function. Today, anesthetics are equal to human anesthetics, which enables your dog to walk out of the clinic the same day as surgery.

Some folks worry about their dogs gaining weight after being neutered or spayed. This is usually not the case. It is true that some dogs may be less active so they could develop a problem, but most are just as active as they were before surgery. However, if your dog should begin to gain, you need to decrease his food and see to it that he gets a little more exercise.

*Toy Poodles are prone to eye problems especially tearing, which is why a little prevention goes a long way.*

## MEDICAL PROBLEMS

### Anal Sacs

Anal sacs are small sacs on either side of the rectum that can cause the dog discomfort when they are full. They should empty when the dog has a bowel movement. Symptoms of inflammation or impaction are excessive licking under the tail and/or a bloody or sticky discharge from the anal area. Breeders recommend emptying the sacs on a regular schedule when bathing the dog. Many veterinarians prefer this isn't done unless there are symptoms. You can express the sacs by squeezing them (at

*Keeping the hair around the eyes well trimmed will decrease irritation.*

the five and seven o'clock positions) in and up toward the anus. Take precautions not to get in the way of the foul-smelling fluid that is expressed. Some dogs object to this procedure, so it would be wise to have someone hold the head. Scooting is caused by anal-sac irritation and not worms.

### Colitis

The stool may be frank blood or blood tinged and is the result of inflammation of the colon. Colitis, sometimes intermittent, can be the result of stress, undiagnosed whipworms, or perhaps idiopathic (no explainable reason). If intermittent bloody stools are an ongoing problem, you should probably feed a diet higher in fiber. Seek professional help if your dog feels poorly and/or the condition persists.

### Conjunctivitis

Many breeds are prone to conjunctivitis. The conjunctiva is the pink tissue that lines the inner surface of the eyeball, except the clear, transparent cornea. Irritating substances such as bacteria, foreign matter, or chemicals can cause it to become reddened and swollen. It is important to keep any hair trimmed from around the eyes. Long hair stays damp and aggravates the problem. Keep the eyes cleaned with warm water and wipe away any matter that has accumulated in the corner of the eyes. If the condition persists, you should see your veterinarian. This problem goes hand in hand with keratoconjunctivitis sicca.

### Ear Infection

Otitis externa is an inflammation of the external ear canal that begins at the outside opening of the ear and extends inward to the eardrum. Dogs with pendulous ears are prone to this disease, but breeds with upright ears also have a high incidence of problems. Allergies, food, and inhalents, along with hormonal problems, such as hypothyroidism, are major contributors to the disease. For those dogs that have recurring problems, you need to investigate the underlying causes if you hope to cure them.

*Don't get any water in your Poodle's ears when bathing him, or he could end up with an ear infection.*

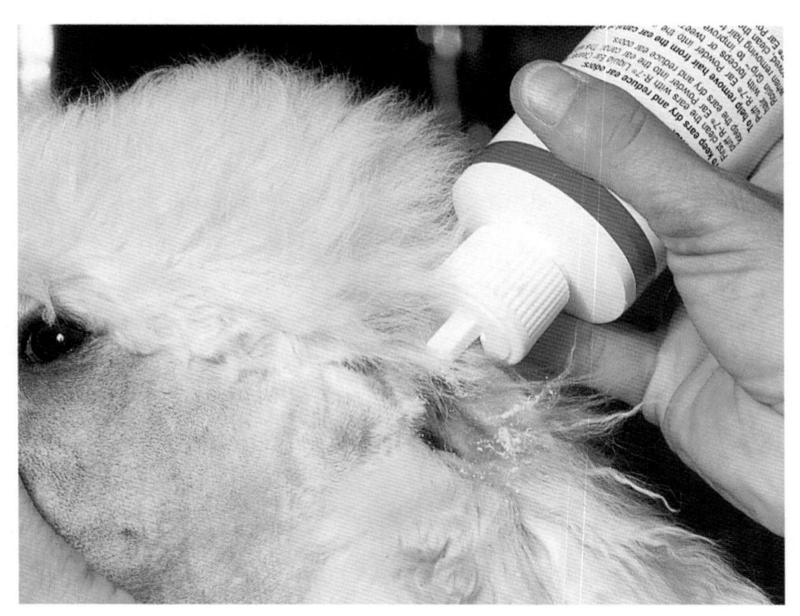

*This Poodle owner applies a special powder to her dog's ears to keep them dry and odor-free.*

Be careful never to get water in the ears. Water provides a great medium for bacteria to grow. If your dog swims or you inadvertently get water in his ears, use a drying agent. You can use an at-home preparation of equal parts of three-percent hydrogen peroxide and 70-percent rubbing alcohol. Another preparation is equal parts of white vinegar and water. Your veterinarian, alternatively, can provide a suitable product. When cleaning the ears, be careful using cotton tip applicators, because they make it easy to pack debris down into the canal. Only clean what you can see.

If your dog has an ongoing infection, don't be surprised if your veterinarian recommends sedating him and flushing his ears with a bulb syringe. Sometimes this needs to be done a few times to get the ear clean. The ear must be clean so that medication can come into contact with the canal. Be prepared to return for rechecks until the infection is gone. This may involve more flushings if the ears are very bad.

For chronic or recurring cases, your veterinarian may recommend thyroid testing, etc., and a hypoallergenic diet for a trial period of 10 to 12 weeks. Depending on your dog, it may be a good idea to see a dermatologist. Ears shouldn't be taken lightly. If the condition gets out of hand, surgery may be necessary. Please ask your veterinarian to explain proper ear maintenance for your dog.

### Flea Bite Allergy

Flea bite allergy is the result of a hypersensitivity to the bite of a flea and its saliva. It only takes one bite to cause the dog to chew or scratch himself raw. Your dog may need medical attention to ease his discomfort. You need to clip the hair around the "hot spot" and wash it with a mild soap and water, and you may need to do this daily if the area weeps. Apply an antibiotic anti-inflammatory product. Hot spots can occur from other trauma, such as grooming.

### Interdigital Cysts

Check for interdigital cysts on your dog's feet if he shows signs of lameness. They are frequently associated with staph infections and can be quite painful. A home remedy is to soak the infected foot in a solution of a half teaspoon of bleach in a couple of quarts of water. Do this two to three times a day for a couple of days. Check with your veterinarian for an alternative remedy; antibiotics usually work well. If there is a recurring

*This Miniature Poodle's regular grooming has kept her flea-free and, consequently, immune from flea bite allergies.*

problem, surgery may be required.

### Lameness

Lameness may only be an interdigital cyst or it could be a mat between the toes, especially if your dog licks his feet. Sometimes it is hard to determine which leg is affected. If your dog is holding up his leg, you need to see your veterinarian.

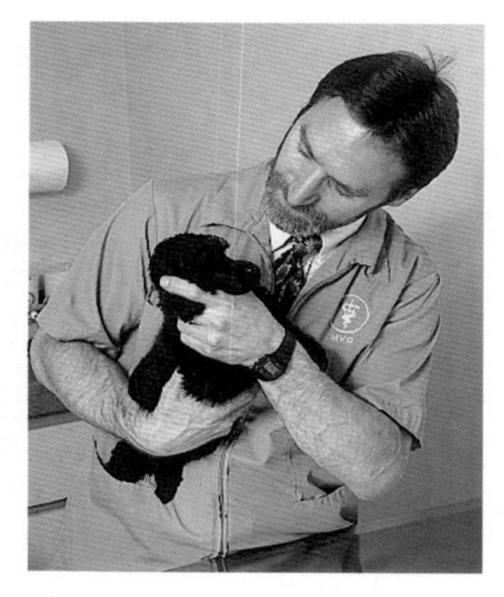

*The importance of consulting a veterinarian on the diagnosis of internal disorders cannot be stressed enough—a relatively common problem could also be a sign of something more serious.*

### Skin

Frequently, poor skin is the result of an allergy to fleas, inhalants, or food. These types of problems usually result in a staph dermatitis. Dogs with food allergies usually show signs of severe itching and scratching. Some dogs with food allergies never once itch. Their only symptom is swelling of the ears with no ear infection. Food allergy may result in recurrent bacterial skin and ear infections. Your veterinarian or dermatologist will recommend a good restricted diet. It is not wise for you to hit and miss with different dog foods. Many of the diets offered over the counter are not the hypoallergenic diet you are led to believe. Dogs acquire allergies through exposure.

Inhalant allergies result in atopy, which causes licking of the feet, scratching the body, and rubbing the muzzle. They may be seasonable. Your veterinarian or dermatologist can perform intradermal testing for inhalant allergies. If your dog should test positive, then a vaccine may be prepared. The results are very satisfying.

### Tonsillitis

Usually, young dogs have a higher incidence of tonsillitis than the older ones. Older dogs have built up resistance. It is very contagious. Sometimes it is difficult to determine if the condition is tonsillitis or kennel cough because the symptoms are similar. Symptoms include fever, poor eating, swallowing with difficulty, and retching up a white, frothy mucus.

# DENTAL CARE for Your Dog's Life

So, you have a new puppy! Anyone who has ever raised a puppy is abundantly aware of how this new arrival affects the household. Your puppy will chew anything he can reach, chase your shoelaces, and play "tear the rag" with any piece of clothing he can find. When puppies are newly born, they have no teeth. At about four weeks of age, puppies of most breeds begin to develop their deciduous or baby teeth. They begin eating semi-solid food, biting and fighting with their littermates, and learning discipline from their mother. As their new teeth come in, they inflict pain on their mother's breasts, so feeding sessions become less frequent and shorter. By six or eight weeks, the mother will start growling to warn her pups when they are fighting too roughly or hurting her as they nurse too much with their new teeth.

*If you train your Poodle to have good chewing habits, he will have healthy teeth through his lifetime.*

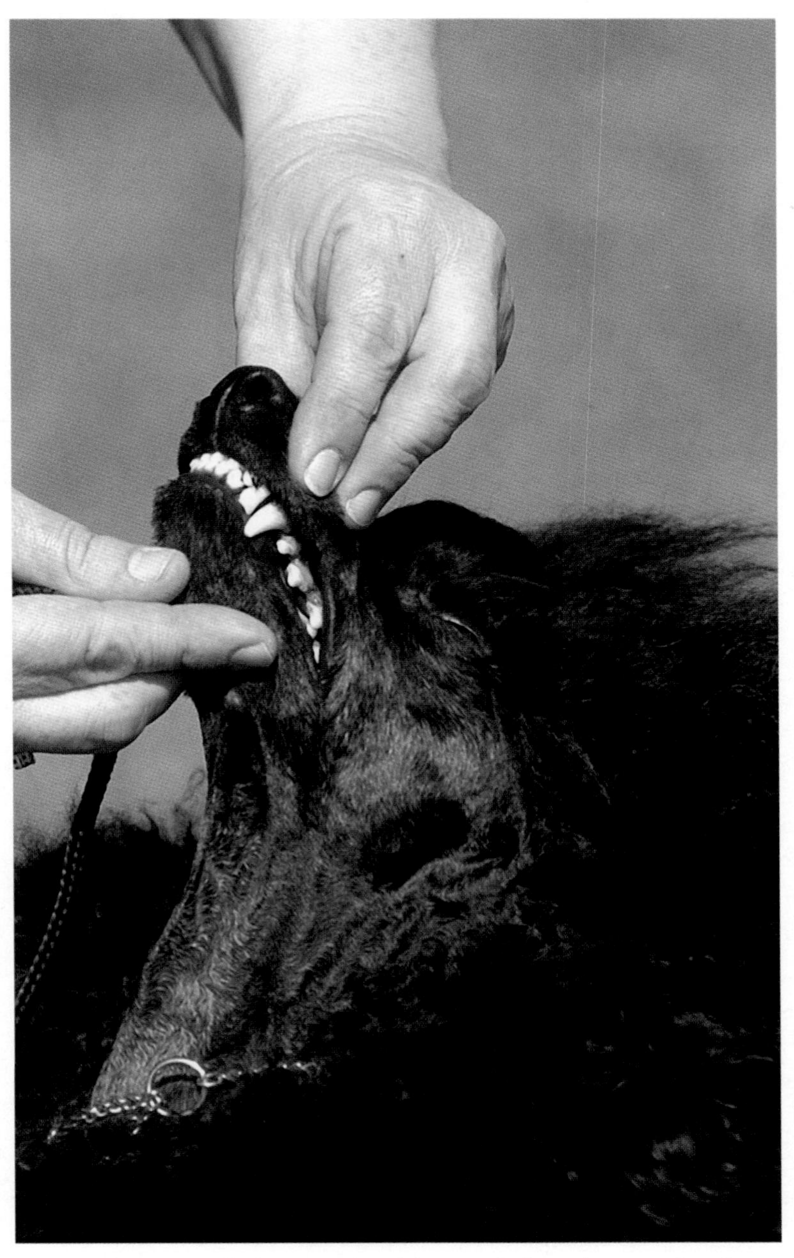

*Dogs, like humans, suffer from periodontal disease, which can destroy teeth and gums.*

Puppies need to chew. It is a necessary part of their physical and mental development. They develop muscles and necessary life skills as they drag objects around, fight over possession, and vocalize alerts and warnings. Puppies chew on things to explore their world. They are using their sense of taste to determine what is food and what is not. How else can they tell an electrical cord from a lizard? At about four months of age, most puppies begin shedding their baby teeth. Often, these teeth need some help to come out to make way for the permanent teeth. The incisors (front teeth) will be replaced first. Then, the adult canine or fang teeth erupt. When a baby tooth is not shed before the permanent tooth comes in, veterinarians call it a retained deciduous tooth. This condition will often cause gum infections by trapping hair and debris between the permanent tooth and the retained baby tooth. Puppies that are given adequate chew toys will exhibit less destructive behavior, develop more physically, and have less chance of retained deciduous teeth.

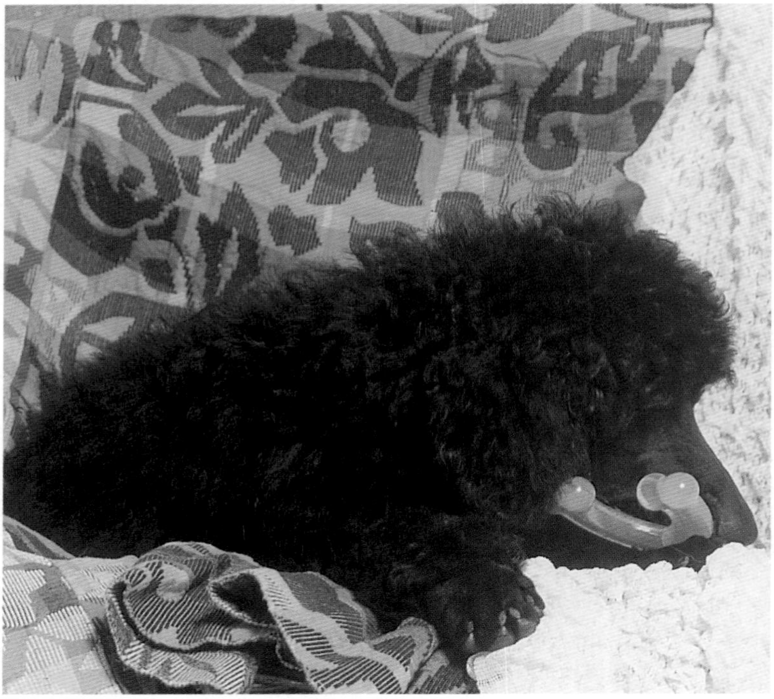

*Puppies need to chew as part of their physical and mental development.*

During the first year, your dog should be seen by your veterinarian at regular intervals. He will let you know when to bring your puppy in for vaccinations and parasite examinations. At each visit, your vet should inspect the lips, teeth, and mouth as part of a complete physical examination. You should take some part in the maintenance of your dog's oral health. Examine your dog's mouth weekly throughout his first year to make sure there are no sores, foreign objects, tooth problems, etc. If your dog drools excessively, shakes his head, or has bad breath, consult your veterinarian. By the time your dog is six months old, his permanent teeth are all in and plaque can start to accumulate on the tooth surfaces. This is when your dog needs good dental-care habits to prevent calculus buildup on his teeth. Brushing is best—that is a fact that cannot be denied. However, some dogs do not like their teeth brushed regularly, or you may not be able to accomplish the task. In this case, you should consider a product that will help prevent plaque and calculus buildup, like any of the dental devices available from Nylabone®.

*Dogs with healthy teeth and gums don't have doggie breath, so everybody loves them.*

By the time dogs are four years old, 75 percent of them have periodontal disease. It is the most common infection in dogs. Yearly examinations by your vet are essential to maintaining your dog's good health. If he detects periodontal disease, he or she may recommend a prophylactic cleaning. To do a thorough cleaning, it will be necessary to put your dog under anesthesia. With modern gas anesthetics and monitoring equipment, the procedure is pretty safe. Your veterinarian will scale the teeth with an ultrasound scaler or hand instrument. This removes the calculus from the teeth. If there are calculus deposits below the gum line, the veterinarian will plane the roots to make them smooth. After all of the calculus has been removed, the teeth are polished with pumice in a polishing cup. If any medical or surgical treatment is needed, it is done at this time. The final step would be fluoride treatment and your follow-

*Nylabones® come in almost as many sizes and colors as Poodles come in.*

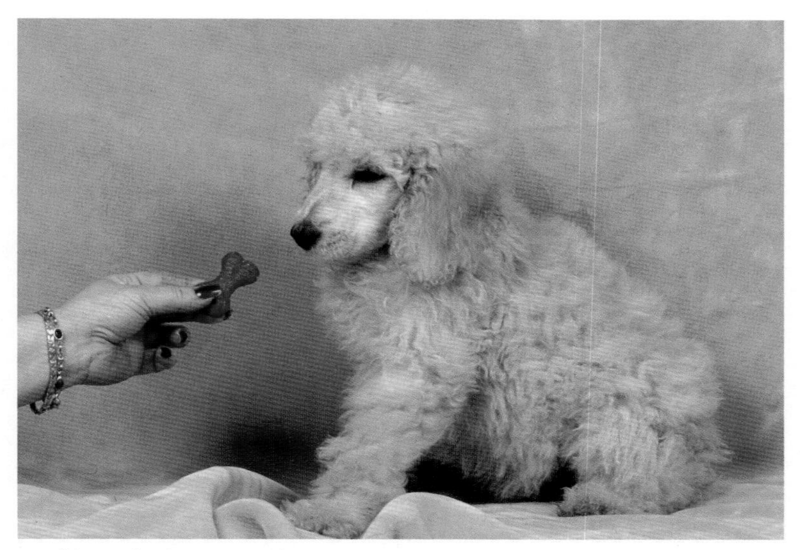

*Healthy and safe treats can be great training motivators.*

up treatment at home. If the periodontal disease is advanced, the veterinarian may prescribe a medicated mouth rinse or antibiotics for use at home. Make sure your dog has safe, clean, and attractive chew toys, like Nylabones®, and healthy treats.

As your dog ages, professional examination and cleaning should become more frequent. The mouth should be inspected at least once a year. Your vet may recommend visits every six months. In the geriatric patient, organs such as the heart, liver, and kidneys do not function as well as when your dog was young. Your vet will probably want to test these organs' functions prior to using general anesthesia for dental cleaning. If your dog is a good chewer and you work closely with your vet, he can keep all of his teeth all of his life. However, as your dog ages, his sense of smell, sight, and taste will diminish. He may not have the desire to chase, trap, or chew his toys. He will also not have the energy to chew for long periods, as arthritis and periodontal disease could make chewing painful. This will leave you with more responsibility for keeping his teeth clean and healthy. The dog that would not let you brush his teeth at one year of age, may let you brush his teeth now that he is ten years old.

If you train your dog with good chewing habits as a puppy, he will have healthier teeth throughout his life.

# IDENTIFICATION and Finding the Lost Dog

There are several ways of identifying your dog. The old standby is a collar with dog license, rabies, and ID tags. Unfortunately, collars have a way of being separated from dogs and tags fall off. We're not suggesting you shouldn't use a collar and tags. If they stay intact and on the dog, they are the quickest form of identification.

For several years, owners have been tattooing their dogs. Some tattoos use a number with a registry. Herein lies the problem, because there are several registries to check. If you wish to tattoo your dog, use your social security number. Humane shelters have the means to trace it. It is usually done on the inside of the rear thigh. The area is first shaved and numbed. There is no pain, although some dogs do not like the buzzing sound. Occasionally, tattooing is not legible and needs to be redone.

*Attaching an identification tag to your Poodle's collar will greatly increase your chances of finding him in case he becomes separated from you.*

The newest method of identification is microchipping. The microchip is a computer chip that is no larger than a grain of rice. The veterinarian implants it by injection between the shoulder blades. The dog feels no discomfort. If your dog is lost and picked up by the humane society, they can trace you by scanning the microchip, which has its own code. Most microchip scanners are friendly to other brands of microchips and their registries. The microchip comes with a dog tag saying that the dog is microchipped. It is the safest way of identifying your dog.

## Finding the Lost Dog

Most people would agree that there would be little worse than losing your dog. Responsible pet owners rarely lose their dogs. They do not let their dogs run free because they don't want harm to come to them. Not only that, but in most, if not all, states there is a leash law.

Beware of fenced-in yards. They can be a hazard. Dogs find ways to escape either over or under fences. Another fast exit may be through the gate that perhaps someone left unlocked.

Below is a list that will hopefully be of help to you if you lose your pet. Remember, don't give up, keep looking. Your dog is worth your efforts.

1. Contact your neighbors and put flyers with a photo on it in their mailboxes. Information you should include would be the dog's name, breed, sex, color, age, source of identification, when your dog was last seen and where, and your name and phone numbers. It may be helpful to say that the dog needs medical care. Offer a *reward.*
2. Check all local shelters daily. It is also possible for your dog to be picked up away from home and end up in an out-of-the-way shelter. Check these, too. Go in person. It is not enough to call. Most shelters are limited on the time they can hold dogs before they are put up for adoption or euthanized. There is the possibility that your dog will not make it to the shelter for several days. He could have been wandering or someone may have tried to keep him.
3. Notify all local veterinarians. Call and send flyers.
4. Call your breeder. Frequently, breeders are contacted when one of their breed is found.
5. Contact the rescue group for your breed.
6. Contact local schools—children may have seen your dog.
7. Post flyers at the schools, groceries, gas stations, convenience stores, veterinary clinics, groomers, and any other places that will allow them.
8. Advertise in the newspaper.
9. Advertise on the radio.

# TRAVELING with Your Dog

The earlier you start traveling with your new puppy or dog, the better. He needs to become accustomed to traveling. However, some dogs are nervous riders and become carsick easily. It is helpful if he starts any trip with an empty stomach. Do not despair, as it will go better if you continue taking him with you on short, fun rides. How would you feel if every time you rode in the car you stopped at the doctor's office for an injection? You would soon dread that nasty car. Older dogs that tend to get carsick may have more of a problem adjusting to traveling. Those dogs that are having serious problems may benefit from medication prescribed by the veterinarian.

Do give your dog a chance to relieve himself before getting into the car. It is a good idea to be prepared for a clean up with a leash, paper towels, bag, and terry cloth towel.

When in the car, the safest place for your dog is in a Nylabone Foldaway Carrier, although close confinement can promote carsickness in some dogs.

An alternative to the crate would be to use a car harness made for dogs and/or a safety strap attached to the harness or collar. Whatever you do, do not let your dog ride in the back of a pickup truck unless he is securely tied on a very short lead. I've seen trucks stop quickly, and, even though the dog was tied, he fell out and was dragged.

*The nice thing about Toy Poodles is they fit into almost anything and can be carried everywhere you go.*

Another advantage of the crate is that it is a safe place to leave your dog if you need to run into the store. Otherwise, you wouldn't be able to leave the windows down. Keep in mind that while many dogs are overly protective in their crates, this may

*This lucky pair of Poodles has its own "pup" tent for a home away from home.*

not be enough to deter dognappers. In some states, it is against the law to leave a dog in the car unattended.

Never leave a dog loose in the car wearing a collar and leash. More than one dog has killed himself by hanging. Do not let him put his head out an open window. Foreign debris can be blown into his eyes. When leaving your dog unattended in a car, consider the temperature. It can take less than five minutes to reach temperatures over 100 degrees Fahrenheit.

## TRIPS

Perhaps you are taking a trip. Give consideration to what is best for your dog—traveling with you or boarding. When traveling by car, van, or motor home, you need to think ahead about locking your vehicle. In all probability you have many valuables in the car and do not wish to leave it unlocked. Perhaps most valuable and not replaceable is your dog. Give thought to securing your vehicle and providing adequate ventilation for him. Another consideration for you when traveling with your dog is medical problems that may arise and little inconveniences, such as exposure to external parasites. Some areas of the country are quite flea infested. You may want to carry flea spray with you. This is even a good idea when staying in motels. Quite possibly you are not the only occupants of the room.

Unbelievably, many motels and even hotels do allow canine guests, even some very first-class ones. Gaines Pet Foods Corporation publishes *Touring With Towser*, a directory of domestic hotels and motels that accommodate guests with dogs. Their address is Quaker Professional Services, PO Box 23-1, Chicago, IL, 60604-9001. Call ahead to any motel that you may be considering and see if they accept pets. Sometimes it is necessary to pay a deposit against room damage. The management may feel reassured if you mention that your dog will be crated. If you do travel with your dog, take along plenty of baggies so that you can clean up after him. When we all do our share in cleaning up, we make it possible for motels to continue accepting our pets. As a matter of fact, you should practice cleaning up everywhere you take your dog.

Depending on where your are traveling, you may need an up-to-date health certificate issued by your veterinarian. It is good policy to take along your dog's medical information, which would include the name, address, and phone number of your veterinarian, vaccination record, rabies certificate, and any medication he is taking.

## AIR TRAVEL

When traveling by air, you need to contact the airlines to check their policy. Usually, you have to make arrangements up to a couple of weeks in advance when traveling with your dog. The airlines require your dog to travel in an airline-approved fiberglass crate. These can be purchased through the airlines, but they are also readily available in most pet-supply stores. If your dog is not

*Show dogs are seasoned travelers who are used to going to competitions around the country.*

accustomed to a crate, it is a good idea to get him acclimated to it before your trip. The day of the actual trip you should withhold water about 1 hour ahead of departure and food for about 12 hours. The airlines generally have temperature restrictions that do not allow pets to travel if it is either too cold or too hot. Frequently, these restrictions are based on the temperatures at the departure and arrival airports. It's best to inquire about a health certificate. These usually need to be issued within ten days of departure. You should arrange for nonstop, direct flights, and if a commuter plane is involved, check to see if it will carry dogs. Some don't. The Humane Society of the United States has put together a tip sheet for airline traveling. You can receive a copy by sending a self-addressed, stamped envelope to:

The Humane Society of the United States
Tip Sheet
2100 L Street NW
Washington, DC 20037.

Regulations differ for traveling outside of the country and are

*This guy is begging to go along. Like most other dogs, Poodles love the companionship of their owners, on and off the road.*